cover photograph	Woodside Station, 1967
	(Colour Rail)
back cover	*Top*, Southport Chapel Street, 1960
	(Colour Rail)
	Bottom, Woodside Station, 1966
	(Colour Rail)
©	Paul Bolger
first published 1994	The Bluecoat Press
	Bluecoat Chambers
	School Lane
	Liverpool L1 3BX
designed by	March design
printed by	Dah Hua Printing Press

ISBN 1 872568 23 8

Acknowledgements
I am indebted to the following people and organisations who contributed photographs, information and observations over a great many years (with apologies to any I may have omitted).

C.A. Appleton, R. Bird, C.E. Box, G. Burgess, H.C. Casserley, R.M. Casserley, F. Dean, P. Gibb, J. Gilmour, K.W. Green, P.H. Hanson, J.B. Hodgson, I.G. Holt, J. Hooper, D. Ibbotson, C.H. Loker, K. Longbottom, B. Mathews, B. Morrison, J.A. Peden, H.B. Priestley, Rev. D. Rokeby, J. Ryan, F.W. Shuttleworth, J.L. Smith, J. Thomlinson, D. Thompson, M. Turner, J. Ward, C. Wilkinson, H. Wilson, Lens of Sutton, Locomotive & General Railway Photographs, National Railway Museum, Stations U.K.

MERSEYSIDE RAILWAY STATIONS & DISTRICT

PAUL BOLGER

The Bluecoat Press

INTRODUCTION

In railway circles photographs of Merseyside's stations are harder to find than from most other regions. No-one knows the reason - the area has had its fair share of enthusiasts after all. When photos do turn up, they always seem to have been taken by people who were resident elsewhere. Perhaps the old saying about never appreciating what you had until after it's gone is part of the answer. In defence of the local enthusiasts, however, it must be said that railways were everywhere in the county and Liverpool in particular. Apart from mainline passenger services there was a multitude of suburban and goods routes, the Liverpool Overhead Railway, the Mersey Docks & Harbour Board lines, the underground Mersey Railway and a seemingly endless list of railway yards and warehouses. Being surrounded by so much they were probably guilty of the assumption that the network would always be there - so what was the point in taking pictures? In addition, the high cost of pre-war photography and the difficulty in obtaining quality film after World War Two are equally valid arguments - had we been in their shoes many of us would have acted no differently. By the time cheap and convenient cameras arrived in the 1960's much of the network had already disappeared.

The point is raised not to apportion blame but to illustrate the difficulties faced by latter day historians when searching for suitable material. The contents of this album have been assembled from all parts of the country and realistically have taken about twenty years to trace. Between the pages you will find in excess of 200 photographs together with relevant information from the 182 railway stations listed.* A number have appeared in other books but a good proportion are very scarce and published here for the first time. Some have come from official sources and picture postcards

but the vast majority are the work of ordinary people who visited this railway Mecca and liked what they saw; roving clergymen, travelling businessmen, servicemen on the move or visiting scholars and relatives. I am immensely grateful that they recorded what so many of us took for granted - I dedicate this collection of photographs to them all. Whilst this is the most comprehensive set of Merseyside station photographs ever published, my search for some stubborn locations continues and I would be delighted to hear from anyone with a picture postcard or photograph of any of the following: Linacre Road, Breck Road, Childwall, Bromborough Port or the small halts at

Formby Power Station, Butts Lane, Heathey Lane, New Cut Lane, Sealand Rifle Range and all three golf club platforms south of the latter.

  * It must be understood that confines of space and the number of venues have greatly dictated the contents of this volume. The term "Merseyside" has been applied without adhesion to metropolitan boundaries in an effort to minimise the severance of routes. Goods only lines have been omitted as have the stations of the Liverpool Overhead Railway - the latter had a tenuous link with the mainline network and its 21 stations would have forced economies elsewhere. Those who require more information on this line may wish to consult my previous

book "THE DOCKER'S UMBRELLA" (Bluecoat Press, 1992) which illustrates the railway at length. Modern day developments such as the Merseyrail system are described in the relevant chapters but not portrayed.

Finally, if visiting the sites of closed stations remember that many buildings have survived as dwellings. Please respect the privacy of the present day occupants and take care not to trespass.

Paul Bolger, 1994

Above *Liverpool Central, 1953.*
Opposite *The Demolition of Liscard & Poulton station in the early 1960's. (Bob Bird)*

THE RAILWAY STATIONS OF MERSEYSIDE & DISTRICT

The opening of the Liverpool & Manchester Railway in 1830, the world's first public iron-road, guaranteed Merseyside a place in the annals of railway history. The growing stature of the port of Liverpool necessitated a quicker and more reliable route for the transport of goods and travellers. Railways grew at the expense of canals and roads and by 1860 a large network of lines had become established.

The Liverpool terminus of the L & M was at Crown Street - a grandiose structure with full canopy and attendant features. The next stations (or "stopping places" as they were then called) in the district were Wavertree Lane, Broad Green, Roby Gate and Huyton Gate - the "Gate" suffixes were later dropped as the areas developed. Stopping place was an apt description as they had no platforms or proper shelter - it was ten years before intermediate stations were recognisable as such. In 1836 a branch from Edge Hill to Liverpool Lime Street was opened, the latter replacing Crown Street as the line's terminus.

The next significant development in the area was the opening of the Chester & Birkenhead Railway in 1840. The original terminus at Birkenhead was Grange Lane being superseded by extensions to Monks Ferry (1844) and Woodside (1878).

However, north of the river was where the growth continued for the next decade as more and more newly formed railway companies sought to share in the lucrative trade of the ever-growing Liverpool dock system. The Liverpool, Crosby & Southport Railway opened a line between Southport Eastbank Street and Waterloo in 1848 (the extension to Southport Chapel Street came in 1851).

The connection to Liverpool was by horse omnibus until the line was extended to Sandhills in 1850 thus connecting with the East Lancashire and Lancashire & Yorkshire Railways courses from Preston and Lostock Junction (near Bolton) to Liverpool Exchange, themselves open by that time (the original section from Lostock Junction to Liverpool Great Howard Street opened in 1848 - the extension to the replacement terminus at Tithebarn Street (later Exchange) came in 1850). The line from Walton Junction was extended north to the Preston area in 1849.

By the end of 1850 a route jointly owned by the Great Western and London & North Western Railways had been opened between Warrington and Chester but another thirteen years would pass before any additions were made to the network south of the Mersey.

The line between Garston Dock and Runcorn was opened by the St. Helens and Runcorn Gap Railway in 1852 and Southport London Road via Burscough Bridge to Wigan followed in 1855.

Hooton and Helsby were connected by rail in 1863 followed by Hooton to Parkgate in 1866, both lines being jointly G.W.R. & L.N.W.R. owned. The Wirral Railway also entered the scene in 1866 with a line from Wallasey Bridge Road (later renamed Birkenhead Docks) to Hoylake - the continuation to West Kirby took another twelve years. The Cheshire Lines Committee Railway reached Helsby and Alvanley in 1869 and a junction to the Hooton - Helsby line was put in in 1871 to enable the company to reach Birkenhead.

The 1860's brought major additions to Liverpool's railway map. The London & North Western Railway opened lines north and south of Edge Hill to Canada Dock and Speke respectively in 1866 and 1864. This latter year also marked the opening of the Garston & Liverpool Railway's line between Garston Dock and Brunswick (it was extended to Liverpool Central a decade later). The North Mersey branch of the Lancashire & Yorkshire railway was opened in 1867 between North Mersey Goods and Fazakerley Junction - although primarily a goods line, passenger services were introduced between Aintree (Sefton Arms) via Ford and Marsh Lane to Liverpool Exchange in 1906 (Gladstone Dock also had a service introduced in 1914).

The L.N.W.R's Canada Dock line was branched to Alexandra Dock in 1880 and a junction with the Liverpool Exchange - Southport Chapel Street route was laid at Bootle (where the rails ran parallel) in 1886. This junction allowed a service between Southport and London Euston (with a connection at Edge Hill). The aforementioned Cheshire Lines Committee (C.L.C.) was a triple-joint line, being owned by the Manchester, Sheffield & Lincolnshire Railway (later known as the Great Central Ry.) and the Great Northern and Midland Railways. The 1870's witnessed an abundance of C.L.C. routes: Cressington to Halewood and beyond opened in 1873, Chester Northgate to Barrow for Tarvin and beyond in 1874, Hunts Cross and Halewood to Walton on the Hill in 1879 and Aintree Central to Huskisson in 1880.

Liverpool's network of lines was more or less complete by 1880 but a great deal of iron-road was still to be laid in the areas of Sefton and the Wirral. The population of these largely rural districts increased as people sought to escape the noisy, grimy conurbations that Liverpool and Birkenhead were becoming. In addition, railways through country areas proved best for the speedy transit of produce, feed and machinery.

Southport contributed to the construction of more lines in Sefton - the two routes already installed (Liverpool 1850 and Wigan 1855) were bringing an increasing number of visitors to the town. It was to become the third largest seaside resort in the country after Brighton and Great Yarmouth as a result of further openings: from the direction of Preston to Southport Windsor Road (later Southport Ash Street) in 1878 - extended to Southport Central in 1882, from Aintree Central to Southport Lord Street in 1884 and from Barton to Meols Cop in 1887. Blackpool rose to prominence much later when Southport's attitude to tourists became more conservative.

As stated earlier, the railways of the Wirral were still to be fully established - a major obstacle in the region's rail development was the river Mersey - the ferries having the monopoly as there was no alternative course. 1886 saw the world's first under-river railway opened, the Mersey Railway, with a link from Liverpool James Street to Green Lane (the extensions to Birkenhead Park, Rock Ferry and Liverpool Central Low Level were opened in 1888, 1891 and 1892 respectively). On the same date in 1888 the Wirral Railway extended its metals with a branch to New Brighton and also linked up with the Mersey Railway at Birkenhead Park. Not only were travellers now able to cross the river quickly and comfortably, the New Brighton seaside was in easy reach of residents both sides of the divide - Chester also became more accessible in 1891 with the opening of the Rock Ferry extension.

A major addition to Liverpool's network was the opening of the Liverpool Overhead Railway in 1893 with extensions in 1894, 1896 and 1905 - it was the world's first elevated electric railway. The city's final passenger route (exempting modern-day developments)

was born of an extension to a goods line between Edge Hill & Waterloo Dock built as far back as 1849! Riverside station was opened in 1895 by the Mersey Docks and Harbour Board to serve boat trains and was connected to the Waterloo goods branch via dockland.

The Hooton to Parkgate line was extended to West Kirby in 1886 and a connection between Chester and Hawarden Bridge (via Sealand) was opened by the Great Central Railway in 1890. The Wirral Railway commenced services to Seacombe in 1895 but the last great development in the area was the Great Central's course from Bidston to a junction with the Chester - Hawarden Bridge line west of Sealand which began operating in 1896.

The pioneering Liverpool & Manchester Railway of 1830 was the precursor to a myriad of passenger routes which served more than 200 stations in the region. This was achieved in 66 years and included no fewer than three world's "firsts". It is sobering to think that a person born in 1820 could easily have witnessed the development from beginning to end and still only have been in their 76th year. Thousands of navvies and horses moved millions of tons of earth and rock - the cost in human and monetary terms was colossal yet only a skeleton of routes remain now, compare the map with today's equivalent for a lesson in what we have lost. The powers that be suggested motor transport was the way forward with door to door access - consider that when next in a 20 mile traffic jam or paying an extortionate price for a parking place far from your intended destination.

A stopping train calls at Gateacre Station in the 1930's. (Lens of Sutton)

LIVERPOOL LIME STREET / CROWN STREET - HUYTON QUARRY

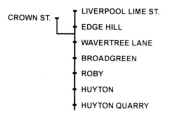

The section between Edge Hill to Huyton Quarry opened on 15th September 1830 as part of the Liverpool & Manchester Railway's line between Liverpool Crown Street and Manchester Liverpool Road. On the 15th August 1836, Lime Street replaced Crown Street as the terminus when a branch from Edge Hill was opened - from that date Crown Street handled goods only. The stations on this section were opened and closed as follows:

	Opened	Closed
LIME STREET	15-8-1836	(still open)
CROWN STREET	15-9-1830	15-8-1836
EDGE HILL	15-8-1836	(still open)
WAVERTREE LANE	pre 2-1831	late 8-1836
BROADGREEN	pre 2-1831	(still open)
ROBY (GATE)	pre 2-1831	(still open)
HUYTON (GATE)	pre 2-1831	(still open)
HUYTON QUARRY	between 2-1831 & 11-1837	15-9-1958

The precise opening dates of intermediate stations such as they were has not survived down the years. A timetable of February 1831 gives the first indications of "Stopping Places" listing Wavertree lane, Broadgreen, Roby Gate and Huyton Gate. At first there were no platforms or amenities at these bleak outposts which sprang up near hamlets or where roads crossed the line - some were near to or at turnpike toll-gates which prompted the suffix. For the first decade of their existence the only shelter, if any, was at gate-keepers' cottages and presumably only then if the resident felt so inclined or was suitably rewarded. The same document makes no mention of Huyton Quarry - the first reference coming in November 1837 when a man was killed near the location.

Wavertree Lane was situated near to the junction of Picton and Spofforth Roads and closed after the substantive station at Edge Hill came into being - the site along with Wavertree Lane itself has long been lost to the maze of surrounding lines. Traffic through the Crown Street tunnel was rope worked by stationary engines - locomotives were detached; coaches were hauled to the terminus and lowered by gravity in the opposite direction.

Edge Hill was known as "New Tunnel" in its early days and, as with Crown Street, rope working (on a reverse gradient) was observed through the tunnel to Lime Street until March 1870 when locomotives took over. By 1881 most of this tunnel had been opened out into cuttings and 1885 saw the line quadrupled. Crown Street station was situated near to the junction with Myrtle Street but the site was later flattened and extended to an area bounded by its namesake, Smithdown Lane and Oxford Street East. It became a coal distribution point and survived in this undignified guise until closure on 1st May 1972.

Huyton Quarry was situated at the east end of Hall Lane near the North View road-bridge.

Above The exterior of Liverpool Lime Street in 1952 clearly showing the original vehicular entrance. Amongst the period advertisements are "Excursion to London - 25/-" (one pound 25 pence) and one depicting the "Gazza" of the day, footballer Stanley Matthews, endorsing Craven A cigarettes! An unthinkable association today. (K.W. Green)

Opposite top Rebuilt "Patriot" class No.45526 Morecambe and Heysham at the head of a train at Lime Street in 1949. (Stations U.K.)

Opposite middle Lime Street's signal box and tunnel mouth in the early 1930's with a "Royal Scot" class engine backing onto a train. (D. Ibbotson)

Opposite bottom Lime Street in 1959 with a "Coronation" class engine awaiting departure in the distance. The days of the steam expresses are numbered however - note the overhead electrified cables and colour-light signal gantries. (H.C. Casserley)

Opposite top left *The original Crown Street tunnel portal looking towards Edge Hill in 1957 - the commemorative notice reads "This tunnel constructed in 1829 by George Stephenson served the original passenger terminus of the Liverpool and Manchester Railway at Crown Street". (A. Appleton)*

Opposite top right *Looking from the tunnel mouth to Edge Hill in the thirties with a host of* milk churns occupying the left hand platform. *(Stations U.K.)*

Opposite middle left *Broad Green station in the 1930's - this is the oldest venue in Liverpool still operating a passenger service having once been part of the Liverpool & Manchester Railway's original line. As will be seen it blossomed into a grand quadruple line station but today the tracks have been* reduced to two once more and the buildings are far less grandiose. *(Stations U.K.)*

Opposite middle right *Roby in 1955 looking east with rebuilt "Patriot" class No.45535 Sir Herbert Walker K.C.B. at the head of a Liverpool-bound train. (Stations U.K.)*

Opposite bottom left *Huyton looking east in 1946. (Stations U.K.)*

Opposite bottom right *A "Black Five" class engine working tender first trundles east with a goods train through Huyton Quarry station in 1946. (Stations U.K.)*

Above *"The Merseyside Express" (ex-Lime Street for London Euston) arrives at Edge Hill in 1959 with "Princess Royal" class No.46203 Princess Margaret Rose in charge. (P.H. Hanson)*

LIVERPOOL EXCHANGE / GREAT HOWARD STREET - BURSCOUGH JUNCTION

	Opened	Closed
GRT HOWARD ST	20-11-1848	13-5-1850
TITHEBARN ST / EXCHANGE	13-5-1850	20-4-1977
SANDHILLS	6-1854	(still open)
KIRKDALE	20-11-1848	(still open)
WALTON JUNCTION	2-4-1849	(still open)
ORRELL PARK	circa 1906	(still open)
AINTREE SEFTON ARMS	2-4-1849	(still open)
OLD ROAN HALT	5-1907	1-10-1909
OLD ROAN	1933	(still open)
MAGHULL	2-4-1849	(still open)
TOWN GREEN & AUGHTON	2-4-1849	(still open)
AUGHTON PARK (HALT)	5-1907	(still open)
ORMSKIRK	2-4-1849	(still open)
BURSCOUGH JUNCTION	2-4-1849	(still open)

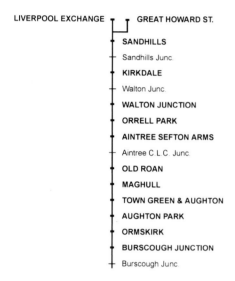

```
LIVERPOOL EXCHANGE ┬─── GREAT HOWARD ST.
                   ├─ SANDHILLS
                   ├─ Sandhills Junc.
                   ├─ KIRKDALE
                   ├─ Walton Junc.
                   ├─ WALTON JUNCTION
                   ├─ ORRELL PARK
                   ├─ AINTREE SEFTON ARMS
                   ├─ Aintree C.L.C. Junc.
                   ├─ OLD ROAN
                   ├─ MAGHULL
                   ├─ TOWN GREEN & AUGHTON
                   ├─ AUGHTON PARK
                   ├─ ORMSKIRK
                   ├─ BURSCOUGH JUNCTION
                   └─ Burscough Junc.
```

Part of Liverpool Exchange concourse in 1934. (Stations U.K.)

The line between Great Howard Street and Walton Junction was opened on 20th November 1848 as part of the railway connecting Liverpool with Lostock Junction (near Bolton). East of Walton Junction was the sole property of the Lancashire & Yorkshire Railway but south to Great Howard Street was jointly operated with the East Lancashire Railway. The said companies extended the line into a replacement terminus at Tithebarn Street on 13th May 1850. This was extensively rebuilt, renamed Liverpool Exchange and partly opened on 12th December 1886 - it was completed on 2nd July 1888. Walton Junction to Burscough Junction was the preserve of the East Lancashire Railway and first saw services on 2nd April 1849.

The East Lancashire and Lancashire & Yorkshire Railways were uneasy bedfellows and could not agree on a common name for either of the joint termini - the former company favoured Great Howard Street over the latter's choice of Borough Gaol in the first case followed by Tithebarn Street and Exchange respectively for the extension. My sympathy goes to the E.L.R. for the first venue as travellers new to the L.Y.R.'s Borough Gaol must have wondered what awaited them at the terminus - the gaol in question was adjacent to the site (being closed on 1st September 1855 with the opening of Walton Prison). The companies amalgamated on 13th August 1859 and were known simply as the L.Y.R. thereafter.

After closure to passengers Great Howard Street became a goods station and remained so until closure on 30th September 1963.

Kirkdale station was known as "Bootle Lane" prior to 1876 and the original name of Sandhills was "North Docks" for the first three years of its existence. Town Green & Aughton was opened as "Town Green", renamed "Town Green & Aughton" on 1st June 1889 but reverted to its original title on 5th May 1975. The original frontage of North Docks station still survives - the bricked-up entrance and window lie on the north footwalk of Sandhills Lane west of the railway bridge.

The first section of this route to be electrified was between Liverpool Exchange and Sandhills Junction as part of the Liverpool - Southport Chapel Street service on 22nd March 1904. It proved a great success and was introduced to the Ormskirk line reaching Aintree on 3rd December 1906, Maghull on 1st October 1909, Town Green & Aughton on 3rd July 1911 and Ormskirk on 1st April 1913.

Primitive stations or "Halts" without platforms were opened at Old Roan and Aughton Park in May 1907 when an economical steam rail-motor service was introduced between Aintree and Ormskirk (refer to the Southport Central / Hillhouse Junction chapter for a photograph of an identical conveyance). Electrification caused the closure of Old Roan (1-10-1909) but Aughton Park was upgraded to a conventional station when the modernised service reached that area (1-4-1913). In 1933 a station proper was opened at Old Roan to meet the demands of the growing population. Closure of the Rainford branch in 1956 precipitated the decline of Ormskirk and the subsequent loss of direct services such as Southport - Ormskirk and Preston

- Liverpool Exchange has reduced the station to a shadow of its former self. The track north of here to Burscough Junction and beyond was singled and the latter now resembles a bus-stop more than a station.

The closure of Liverpool Exchange marked the beginning of a new chapter in the region's rail history - on 2nd May 1977 an extension opened to new stations at Moorfields (Low Level) and Liverpool Central (Low Level). The old L.Y.R. site was bypassed and the line plunged underground to join the Low-Level part of the newly constructed "Merseyrail" system. This allowed connections with the ex-Mersey Railway underground line (itself part of the new network having been looped and renamed Deep-Level) and an end-on link with the ex-Cheshire Lines Committee Railway's route to Hunts Cross. Thus, the Liverpool - Ormskirk line presently forms part of the "Northern Line" of Merseyrail together with Liverpool - Kirkby and Southport - Hunts Cross.

Top left *Liverpool Exchange from Tithebarn Street in the 1920's. (Stations U.K.)*

Top right *Looking towards the buffer-stops at Liverpool Exchange in 1965 with a local electric waiting its next turn. (Stations U.K.)*

Above *An elevated view of the L.Y.R. terminus from Exchange Hotel which backed on to the concourse. (J. Ryan collection)*

Opposite top left Sandhills in 1965 looking towards Liverpool. (Stations U.K.)

Opposite top right A 1930's view of Kirkdale station looking north. (Stations U.K.)

Opposite middle left B.R. Standard class 4 No.75026 calls at Walton Junction on 12th May 1965 with the 14.55 Preston to Liverpool Exchange service. (I.G. Holt)

Opposite middle right Orrell Park station was opened circa 1906 as a direct result of

the success of the electrification between Sandhills and Aintree which introduced a more frequent and rapid local service. This view, taken about 1910, looks north. (Stations U.K.)

Opposite bottom left Orrell Lane, Liverpool in 1928 with the Orrell Park station ticket office right of centre. (Liverpool City Engineers Dept.)

Opposite bottom right A pre-electrification

view of Aintree (Sefton Arms) looking south and before the introduction of the overall canopy to platform 1 (left). (B. Mathews collection)

Above Looking north to Aintree Sefton Arms on Grand National day in the early 1950's. The train nearest the camera is a Liverpool Overhead Railway excursion having just deposited its passengers on platform 3. This and platform 4 (left of same and not in

view) were generally only used on race-days to accommodate extra traffic but number 3 did play host to trains on the Aintree / Liverpool Exchange (via Ford and Marsh Lane) service prior to cessation in 1951. (C.E. Box)

15

Right top The entrance to Old Roan station on the Liverpool-bound side a few years after opening. (Stations U.K.)

Right bottom A beautiful close-up of a L.Y.R. train with staff at Maghull station taken no doubt to celebrate the extension of electrified services to that area in 1909. (Stations U.K.)

Opposite top left A 1905 pre-electric view of Town Green & Aughton looking north. (Stations U.K.)

Opposite top right Looking south to Aughton Park Halt circa 1910. Platforms were not entirely necessary here at that time as the only stopping service was a small steam-railmotor whose coach was equipped with folding steps (see Barton station for a photo of an identical conveyance). (Stations U.K.)

Opposite middle left Aughton Park in 1950 looking north. (Stations U.K.)

Opposite middle right Ormskirk station as viewed from the Derby Street bridge around 1910 - the finely garbed passengers would suggest it is a Sunday. (B. Mathews collection)

Opposite bottom left "Black Five" class No.45464 at the head of a Blackpool - Liverpool Exchange train whilst stopped at Ormskirk in 1962. Workings through Ormskirk are not operated today, the station having become a terminus for trains from both directions. (I.G. Holt)

Opposite bottom right Burscough Junction in 1957 looking south as an ex-Liverpool Exchange service eases into the platform. Today the line has been singled and the facilities reduced to no more than "bus stop" appearance. (H.C. Casserley)

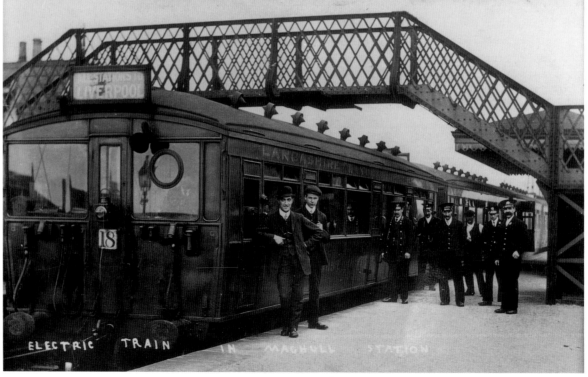

SOUTHPORT CHAPEL STREET - SANDHILLS JUNCTION

The first portion of this route to open was the Liverpool, Crosby & Southport Railway's single line between Waterloo and Southport Eastbank Street on 21st July 1848. Horse omnibuses completed the connection to Liverpool until 1st October 1850 when the line was extended south to meet the joint East Lancashire and Lancashire & Yorkshire Railways at Sandhills Junction. The railway was extended north to a replacement terminus at Southport Chapel Street on 22nd August 1851 and the whole line absorbed by the L.Y.R. in 1855.

	Opened	Closed
SOUTHPORT CHAPEL ST.	22-8-1851	(still open)
SOUTHPORT EASTBANK ST.	21-7-1848	22-8-1851
BIRKDALE	1851	(still open)
HILLSIDE	5-1926	(still open)
AINSDALE	21-7-1848	(still open)
FRESHFIELD	c 4-1854	(still open)
FORMBY	21-7-1848	(still open)
FORMBY POWER STATION	c 1917	c 1944
ALTCAR RIFLE RANGE	1862	c 10-1893
	reopened c 4-1894	3-10-1921
HIGHTOWN	21-7-1848	(still open)
HALL ROAD	1874	(still open)
BLUNDELLSANDS & CROSBY	21-7-1848	(still open)
WATERLOO	21-7-1848	(still open)
SEAFORTH & LITHERLAND	1-10-1850	(still open)
MARSH LANE & STRAND RD	c 11-1850	(still open)
BOOTLE VILLAGE	c 11-1850	c 4-1876
BOOTLE ORIEL ROAD	c 4-1876	(still open)
MILLERS BRIDGE	12-1850	c 4-1876
BANK HALL	1870	(still open)

The line was single track until doubled in 1852 and electric services were introduced on 22nd March 1904. The success of the latter resulted in the number of daily trains rising from 76 to 131 and led the Lancashire & Yorkshire Railway to electrify the Ormskirk line.

Formby station opened as "Formby & Altcar", the suffix being dropped circa January 1866. Altcar Rifle Range was known as "Hightown Rifle Station" until July 1886 and the original name of Blundellsands & Crosby was simply "Crosby" being renamed "Crosby & Blundellsands" on 1st June 1852 reversing to "Blundellsands & Crosby" in June 1878. Seaforth & Litherland was "Seaforth" prior to 1905 and Marsh Lane & Strand Road was originally "Marsh Lane & Linacre" before renaming to "Marsh Lane & Strand Road" and "Bootle New Strand" on 11th April 1886 and 1966 respectively - the former when the station (north of Marsh Lane) was resited sandwiched between those two thoroughfares. Its final name was in recognition of the large shopping complex opened nearby. Birkdale was renamed "Birkdale Park" in April 1854 but reverted to its original title about April 1965.

Waterloo was at first sited alongside Brighton Road with a level crossing for South Road - the present station (south of the road) was built in 1880/1 when a roadbridge was erected. Blundellsands & Crosby underwent a similar relocation in 1881 when the original venue at a level crossing on Mersey Road was abandoned in favour of its present position further north. A roadbridge was put in at Mersey Road and travellers over same today can just see the roof-top of the former stationmaster's house.

Southport Chapel Street reached its fullest extent in 1914 when it enveloped the land hitherto occupied by the East Lancashire Railway's terminus in London Street. Having been deemed unsafe, the grandiose frontage at Chapel Street was replaced by the present building in 1970/1.

Hall Road's origin is a testimony to the determination of wealthy merchant, Joseph Gardner. He asked the railway company to built a station and thus save him a long walk to Blundellsands - predictably they declined stating another five houses would have to exist before consideration could be given. Mr. Gardner duly had them built and a stunned L.Y.R. conceded defeat. Two tragic accidents occurred on the line in Edwardian days - the first on 15th July 1903 when a Southport-bound express derailed and mounted the platform at Waterloo killing eight people and injuring a further twenty. Worse was to come on 27th July 1905 at Hall Road when a northbound express ploughed into an empty train and claimed the lives of twenty-one passengers with another forty-five injured.

The small halt for workers at Formby Power Station stood south of Hogshill Lane and just north of the River Alt. Altcar Rifle Range was situated a third of a mile north of Hightown and was equipped with a bay platform for the exchange of munitions to a small tramway which supplied the nearby ranges. Bootle Village was south of Merton Road as was Millers Bridge of its namesake prior to both being replaced by the intermediate Bootle Oriel Road.

Right Southport Chapel Street from the air in September 1967 - the line to Liverpool curves off to the left whilst the Preston and Wigan tracks veer bottom right. Southport engine shed which closed the previous year can also be seen bottom right (now "Steamport" transport museum). (C.H. Loker)

SOUTHPORT CHAPEL ST.
SOUTHPORT EASTBANK ST.
BIRKDALE
HILLSIDE
AINSDALE
FRESHFIELD
FORMBY
FORMBY POWER STN.
ALTCAR RIFLE RANGE
HIGHTOWN
HALL ROAD
BLUNDELLSANDS & CROSBY
WATERLOO
SEAFORTH & LITHERLAND
Marsh Lane Junc.
MARSH LANE & STRAND ROAD
BOOTLE VILLAGE
BOOTLE ORIEL ROAD
MILLERS BRIDGE
Bootle Junc.
BANK HALL
Sandhills Junc.

Opposite top left Class 3 tank engine No.40195 stands inside Southport Chapel Street (platform 8) at the head of a stopping train to Preston in 1956.
(National Railway Museum)

Opposite top right Alongside the entrance to the Telegraph Office at Chapel Street was a splendid departure board of typical L.Y.R. design complete with adjustable enamelled plates which gave times of trains and platform numbers under various destination headings. The photograph was certainly taken after 1938 as the Downholland (see Barton) column is devoid of any times.
(National Railway Museum)

Opposite middle left An electric for Liverpool Exchange stands at Chapel Street No.2 in 1954. (Stations U.K.)

Opposite middle right Birkdale station looking south in 1954 - note the extent of canopy cover then. (Stations U.K.)

Opposite bottom left The newest of all the stations on the Southport / Liverpool Exchange line was Hillside seen here from a southerly viewpoint in 1965. (Stations U.K.)

Opposite bottom right Ainsdale looking south from the level crossing in 1949.
(Stations U.K.)

Left top Looking north to Freshfield from the footbridge in Edwardian days.
(B. Mathews collection)

Left bottom Formby station in L.Y.R. days and prior to the provision of the road overbridge which replaced the level crossing shown here. Note the boards which instruct waiting passengers where to stand for their preferred compartment: First Class Smoking, First Class Non-Smoking, Third Class Smoking and Third Class Non-Smoking. Whilst you may think this was merely in keeping with the courtesy of that time, don't forget it was in everybody's interest that passengers boarded quickly - twenty seconds lost at each of the fifteen intermediate stations would add 5 minutes to the journey time and seriously disrupt schedules which were tight during peak periods when expresses ran also.
(Stations U.K.)

Below *Altcar Rifle Range station circa 1910, looking north. (Lens of Sutton)*

Bottom left *An early view of Hightown station looking south. Today a footbridge has replaced the level crossing shown here which was made redundant following the construction of an overbridge further north. (Stations U.K.)*

Bottom right *Hall Road looking north from the level crossing in the 1920's. (Stations U.K.)*

Opposite top left *Blundellsands & Crosby station circa 1910 with a stopping train for Liverpool Exchange. (Stations U.K.)*

Opposite top right *Waterloo, circa 1912, with an obliging porter loading a patron's bicycle in the goods locker - trains today have no such facility and passengers have to share with prams and other contraptions, space permitting. (Stations U.K.)*

Opposite middle left *An overall view of Seaforth & Litherland from the south in 1938. Stations from here to Liverpool Exchange had four platforms to accommodate additional lines made necessary by the extra traffic to and from its dockland connections. (C.E. Box)*

Opposite middle right *Looking north to Marsh Lane & Strand Road in 1965. This station was completely destroyed in the May 1941 blitz and only rebuilt with platforms for three of the four running lines as seen here. (Stations U.K.)*

Opposite bottom left *Bootle Oriel Road station from the south in 1965. (Stations U.K.)*

Opposite bottom right *Bank Hall in 1965 with its two island platforms. In earlier days the canopy cover reached right up to the photographer's standpoint - today the canopies have gone and urban redevelopment has reclaimed the right hand platform. (Stations U.K.)*

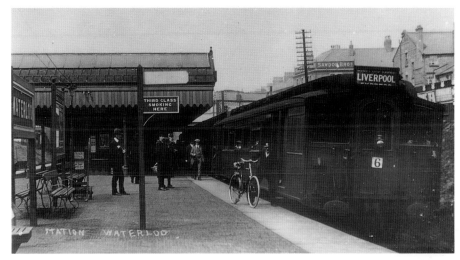

SOUTHPORT CHAPEL ST. / SOUTHPORT LONDON ST. - BURSCOUGH BRIDGE

The Southport London Street site was absorbed in the Chapel Street expansion of 1914 but its name did live on in a small capacity with the provision of the "London Street Excursion Platforms" which handled the bulk of holiday traffic - in reality though they were actually Nos. 12 & 13 of Chapel Street. The site today is occupied by the inevitable car park.

St. Lukes opened as "Barton Street", was renamed "Southport (St. Lukes Road)" circa October 1883, "Southport (St. Lukes)" on 1st March 1902 and finally "St. Lukes" about May 1914. It absorbed the nearby Ash Street station in June 1902 and began serving the Preston line also (this line was electrified from Southport to Crossens from 22nd March 1904). As indicated earlier the station was closed in two parts - for the purposes of this chapter, it is the earlier one which concerns us most. Few traces of the station remain which was situated on Rose Hill.

Blowick was originally known as "Cop End" until 1st October 1871 and was on the section which closed to all traffic on 14th June 1965 (St. Lukes Junction to Pool Hey Junction). From this date all Southport / Wigan traffic was rerouted via Meols Cop station and Pool Hey Junction. Nothing remains of Blowick today - it stood on Meols Cop Road north of the school with a platform either side of the level crossing.

Bescar Lane had the distinction of being the lowest station on the L.Y.R. network at just 12.5 feet above sea-level.

```
SOUTHPORT LONDON ST.
(SOUTHPORT CHAPEL ST.)
    ├─ St. Lukes Junc.
    ├─ ST. LUKES
    ├─ BLOWICK
    ├─ Pool Hey Junc.
    ├─ BESCAR LANE
    ├─ NEW LANE
    ├─ BURSCOUGH BRIDGE
    └─ Burscough Junc.
```

This joint Lancashire & Yorkshire and East Lancashire Railways section was opened on 9th April 1855 as part of the Southport to Wigan service - beyond Burscough Bridge the line was owned solely by the L.Y.R. Chapel Street was the terminus for the L.Y.R. with the adjacent London Street serving E.L.R. services until 1st April 1857 when it became a goods depot. From this date all trains were operated from Chapel Street. The companies amalgamated on 13th August 1859.

	Opened	Closed
SOUTHPORT LONDON ST.	9-4-1855	1-4-1857
ST. LUKES	2-7-1883	14-6-1965[1]
BLOWICK	early 1871	25-9-1939
BESCAR LANE	9-4-1855	(still open)
NEW LANE	9-4-1855	(still open)
BURSCOUGH BRIDGE	9-4-1855	(still open)

[1]Southport / Wigan platforms only (completely closed 8-9-1968).

Opposite top *Southport London Street excursion platforms in 1965 which occupied land hitherto used as the approach to the old East Lancashire Railway terminus at London Street. As mentioned in the main text these two platforms (numbered 12 & 13) were really an annexe of Southport Chapel Street, seen in the distance, which absorbed the E.L.R. site in 1914. (Stations U.K.)*

Opposite middle *Looking east to the Wigan platforms of St. Lukes in 1954 as an unidentified "Black Five" class eases into the platform with a stopping train. (Stations U.K.)*

Opposite bottom *St. Lukes (Wigan line) in 1957 taken from the opposite direction. (H.C. Casserley)*

Left top *The platforms at Blowick were staggered either side of the level crossing. This view taken about 1910 shows the eastbound portion with a steam railmotor (ex-Ormskirk) approaching the photographer. (Stations U.K.)*

Left bottom *A diesel multiple unit for Southport passing the site of Blowick station in 1964 - less than a year before this stretch of line was abandoned. (Stations U.K.)*

Right top *Looking east to Bescar Lane station in 1963. (Stations U.K.)*
Right bottom *New Lane station as viewed from the level crossing in 1963. (Stations U.K.)*
Opposite *Burscough Bridge in L.Y.R. days looking east. (P. Gibb collection)*

LIVERPOOL CENTRAL - HALEWOOD

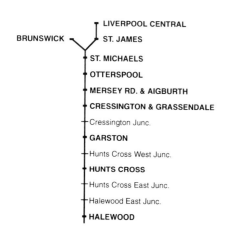

Brunswick to Cressington Junction opened on 1st June 1864 as part of the Garston & Liverpool Railway's line between Brunswick and Garston Junction - it was absorbed by the Cheshire Lines Committee Railway on 5th July 1865. Coaches conveyed patrons between the terminus and the company offices in Lower Castle Street, Liverpool until the extension to Central was opened on 2nd March 1874 - Brunswick then closed and the site was incorporated into the surrounding goods complex. The section between Cressington Junction and Halewood opened to passengers on 1st August 1873 as part of the C.L.C. line between Cressington Junction and Skelton West Junction.

	Opened	Closed
LIVERPOOL CENTRAL	2-3-1874	17-4-1972
ST. JAMES	2-3-1874	1-12-1916
BRUNSWICK	1-6-1864	2-3-1874
ST. MICHAELS	1-6-1864	17-4-1972
reopened	3-1-1978	(still open)
OTTERSPOOL	1-6-1864	5-3-1951
MERSEY RD. & AIGBURTH	1-6-1864	17-4-1972
reopened	3-1-1978	(still open)
CRESSINGTON & GRASS.	1-3-1873	17-4-1972
reopened	3-1-1978	(still open)
GARSTON	1-4-1874	17-4-1972
reopened	3-1-1978	(still open)
HUNTS CROSS	5-1874	(still open)
HALEWOOD	5-1874	17-9-1951

The section between Hunts Cross West Junction to a point just south of Liverpool Central (closed 14-7-1972) was given a new lease of life on 3rd January 1978 when it reopened with electric traction to form part of the "Northern Line" of Merseyrail. With the addition of a new connection via Moorfields to Sandhills, it began operating a through service between Hunts Cross and Southport.

Otterspool was spelled "Otter's Pool" until April 1866, Mersey Road & Aigburth was simply "Mersey Road" prior to 1880 but became "Aigburth" after Merseyrail reopened. Cressington & Grassendale was "Cressington" prior to January 1877 and reverted to this singular title on 3rd January 1978. Hunts Cross was rebuilt in 1883 to accommodate the quadrupling of lines between there and Halewood East Junction - today, however, the main line has been reduced to double track once more since the removal of the once busy Halewood Junctions which gave access to Huskisson and Southport.

The site of Liverpool Central is now occupied by a shopping complex but the platforms of St. James station (in a deep cutting under Ashwell Street) are still visible from passing trains. Brunswick was situated on Sefton Street south of its junction with Northumberland Street but nothing remains today. Otterspool station stood at the end of a lane from Aigburth Vale and the main

building has survived as a private dwelling. Halewood stood on the north side of Bailey's Lane but all traces have since disappeared.

Above *Liverpool Central exterior in 1955. (National Railway Museum)*

Opposite top *Stanier "Mogul" class No.42949 standing at the head of a Liverpool Central - Stockport service in August 1955. (B. Morrison)*

Opposite bottom left *The magnificent single-span at Liverpool Central is shown to good effect in this 1965 view from the concourse. The descending staircase on the left provided a connection to the low-level station which took passengers on to the Wirral and Chester. (Stations U.K.)*

Opposite bottom right *As with Lime Street, the approaches to Liverpool Central were entirely in tunnel - this 1947 photograph shows the tracks disappearing into the same beyond the end of the platform. The engine in the distance is standing in the cramped loco yard having just been watered and turned in readiness for its next duty. (C. Wilkinson)*

Opposite top The original terminal building at Brunswick, still standing in 1971 after almost a hundred years of closure, is dwarfed by the massive C.L.C. goods warehouse which built up around it. (J.F. Ward)

Opposite bottom left The dark and satanic remains of St. James station in the mid-thirties looking towards Brunswick. (D. Ibbotson)

Opposite bottom right Looking southeast to St. Michaels station in 1971, the year before its initial closure. (Stations U.K.)

Top left Otterspool station from the west around 1910. (Stations U.K.)

Top right A great variety of enamel advertising signs and railway posters adorn Mersey Road in this view looking towards Otterspool around 1910. (Stations U.K.)

Bottom left Mersey Road from the roadbridge in the 1930's. (Stations U.K.)

Bottom right Cressington & Grassendale looking east in 1971 - beyond the bridge lies Cressington Junction whose right fork once served Garston (Central) Goods depot and led to an end-on junction with the ex-London & North Western Railway at that company's Garston Dock (passenger) station. (Stations U.K.)

Right top *This 1950 view shows the once grand exterior of Garston (Cheshire Lines) station. (H.C. Casserley)*

Right bottom *Looking east to Garston, circa 1910 with coaches occupying the loop line. (J. Ryan collection)*

Opposite top *Hunts Cross in the 1930's looking towards Liverpool. Note the four platforms and beautiful Victorian cast iron urinal right of centre. (Stations U.K.)*

Opposite bottom *An eastbound express roaring through Halewood about 1910. (Stations U.K.)*

EDGE HILL - SPEKE / GARSTON

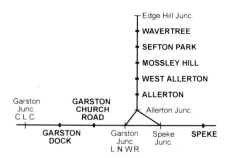

Garston Dock to Speke first saw services on 1st July 1852 as part of the St. Helens & Runcorn Gap Railway's route between Runcorn and Garston. This company was absorbed by the London & North Western Railway on 29th July 1864 after the latter opened its link between Edge Hill Junction and Speke Junction earlier that year (15th February). A curve connecting Allerton and Garston was opened on New Year's Day, 1873 which allowed direct running between Garston and Edge Hill.

	Opened	Closed
WAVERTREE	9-1870	5-8-1958
SEFTON PARK	6-1892	2-5-1960
MOSSLEY HILL	15-2-1864	(still open)
WEST ALLERTON	2-1-1939	(still open)
ALLERTON	15-2-1864	(still open)
GARSTON DOCK	1-7-1852	15-4-1917
reopened 5-5-1919		16-6-1947
GARSTON CHURCH RD	1-3-1881	15-4-1917
reopened 5-5-1919		3-7-1939
SPEKE	1-7-1852	22-9-1930

Edge Hill Junction to Speke and beyond was quadrupled on 13th July 1891 and in the process Mossley Hill station was moved further north. Its formal title was "Mossley Hill for Aigburth" with Allerton once known as "Allerton for Garston".

Wavertree and Sefton Park stations stood on the south sides of Wellington and Smithdown Roads respectively whilst Speke was situated at Woodend Lane (now called Woodend Avenue). Garston Dock could be found on the east side of Dock Road and, predictably, the neighbouring Garston Church Road was west of its namesake.

Right top Wavertree looking south in the year of closure - 1958. Platforms three and four are visible to the left with a stopping train for Lime Street awaiting the all-clear at No.3. (Stations U.K.)

Right middle An unidentified "Patriot" class heads a train south through Sefton Park in 1958. (Stations U.K.)

Right bottom "Britannia" class No.70033 Charles Dickens with an ex-Lime Street express passing through West Allerton in the early 1960's. (I.G. Holt)

Opposite top left Looking north to the twin island platforms at Mossley Hill (for Aigburth) in 1949. (Stations U.K.)

Opposite top right Station staff and friends posing at Mossley Hill around 1909. (J. Ryan collection)

Opposite bottom Sefton Park in 1958 looking south. (Stations U.K.)

Right top *Allerton (for Garston) looking northwest circa 1930. (Stations U.K.)*

Right bottom *Garston Dock station in the 1920's from the south. Beyond the crossover are large swing barriers (shown closed here) which marked the end-on junction with the Cheshire Lines Committee's metals further on. When opened, it was possible to connect with that company's line to Liverpool Central. (Stations U.K.)*

Opposite top *The other ex-L.N.W.R. station in the Garston area was Garston Church Road shown here in the 1920's looking southeast. (Stations U.K.)*

Opposite bottom *Speke station in L.N.W.R. days looking west from an embankment. (Stations U.K.)*

EDGE HILL - CANADA DOCK / ALEXANDRA DOCK

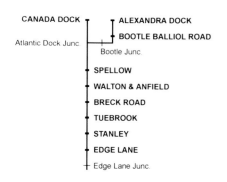

Services between Edge Hill and Tuebrook commenced on 1st June 1866 with the line extending to Canada Dock later the same year for goods traffic - passenger trains did not work the whole route until 1st July 1870. The satellite branch from Atlantic Dock Junction to Alexandra Dock carried its first commuters on 5th September 1881 and Bootle Junction (to the L.Y.R. Liverpool - Southport line) was opened on 1st May 1886. The latter allowed through services between Southport and Edge Hill with a connection for the Liverpool - London expresses.

	Opened	Closed
EDGE LANE	11-1870	31-5-1948[1]
STANLEY	1-6-1866	31-5-1948[1]
TUEBROOK	1-6-1866	31-5-1948
BRECK ROAD	1-7-1870	31-5-1948[1]
WALTON & ANFIELD	1-7-1870	31-5-1948[1]
SPELLOW	9-1882	31-5-1948
CANADA DOCK	1-7-1870	5-5-1941
BOOTLE BALLIOL ROAD	5-9-1881	31-5-1948[1]
ALEXANDRA DOCK	5-9-1881	31-5-1948[1]

[1]Services were suspended from this date (except for through Southport / Edge Hill trains) and closure was declared on 26th February 1949 - however, the effective date of closure was 31st May 1948 as stopping trains were never reinstated. It is worth noting that the through services, latterly with diesel railcars, survived until 9th October 1977.

Alexandra Dock opened as "Atlantic Dock" but was renamed on 10th September 1881 and Bootle Balliol Road was simply "Balliol Road" prior to 1st January 1891. Canada Dock was known as "Bootle" until 5th September 1881 and Walton & Anfield's original title was "Walton for Aintree" up to 1st January 1910.

Canada Dock was a war-time casualty - its closure was brought about by flooding when a bomb breached a nearby canal aqueduct. Although it never reopened, the station survived intact until December 1992 when the area was redeveloped. It stood on the east side of Derby Road just south of the junction with Bankhall Street.

With the exception of the Canada Dock spur, the line is still open and serves the Seaforth container base at Liverpool Freeport. Contrary to what one might expect with the passage of forty-five years, there is still ample evidence of three of the stations. Platforms or mounds are still in evidence at Balliol Road, Spellow and Walton & Anfield with buildings extant at Balliol Road and Spellow. The booking hall of the former stands on Oriel Road opposite Bootle Town Hall and the latter is now a book-makers but many will remember it as "Kelly's Furnishers" prior to this.

Alexandra Dock stood on Regent Road (north of Nelson Street), Walton & Anfield was south of Walton Lane (by Cherry Lane), Breck Road north of Townsend Lane, Stanley on the north side of Prescot Road (near Prescot Drive) and Edge Lane was situated south of its namesake (east of Binns Road).

Opposite Edge Lane station just prior to closure in 1948 from the road of the same name. During the Second World War this line played a leading role in supplying the nation - note the number of triangular concrete vehicle obstructions still in situ on the opposite embankment. They would not have expected tanks this far inland so I can only surmise they were to deter saboteurs from rolling obstructions onto the line. (Stations U.K.)

Top left A southbound freight passing through Stanley station in the 1930's. (Stations U.K.)

Top right Tuebrook looking south between the wars with the massive Liverpool Corporation electric generating station visible in the distance. (Stations U.K.)

Bottom left Walton & Anfield from the Walton Lane bridge prior to 1910 whilst still known as "Walton for Aintree". With the district of Aintree almost two miles away to the north, this is proof of how some station names could mislead the traveller. The amendment to "Anfield" was probably as a direct result of complaints from leg weary patrons who had taken the name at face value. (Stations U.K.)

Bottom right Spellow station was in a deep cutting as will be seen from this early 1920's view looking west. Close inspection of the posters on the opposite platform reveal no fewer than eleven on three large L.N.W.R. boards. (Stations U.K.)

Right top Looking towards the buffers at Canada Dock's single platform in 1959 on the occasion of an enthusiast's visit - although closing eighteen years previous (see notes), the station is intact including the platform nameboard. (R.M. Casserley)

Right bottom Bootle Balliol Road lay beneath Millers Bridge which this 1951 view looking south shows. (Stations U.K.)

Opposite The other passenger terminal on this branch was at Alexandra Dock - in this 1959 view from Derby Road we see it playing host to a specially chartered enthusiasts' train. Like Canada Dock station, Alexandra had survived more or less intact despite years of closure. (R.M. Casserley)

KIRKBY - WALTON JUNCTION / GLADSTONE DOCK

The line between Walton Junction and Kirkby was opened by the Lancashire & Yorkshire Railway on 20th November 1848 as part of the route from Liverpool to Lostock Junction (near Bolton). Fazakerley Junction to Gladstone Dock began life as a L.Y.R. freight line to North Mersey Goods (by Hornby Dock) in August 1867 - the first passenger trains to tread the branch did so from 1st June 1906 between Mersey Branch Junction and Sefton Junction as part of an electrified service from Liverpool Exchange to Aintree via Marsh Lane. Liverpool Overhead Railway trains began running to Aintree in the same year (via Rimrose Junction) and the L.Y.R. electrified service was extended to a newly constructed single platformed station at Gladstone Dock on 7th September 1914. Racecourse station was added circa 1890 for Grand National excursion traffic and was of curious design - the eastbound trackbed was raised to act as a platform for passengers alighting from trains on the opposite line (see photograph).

Fazakerley was named "Simonswood" until 1850 and "Aintree" until 1860. Racecourse was known as "Aintree Cinder Lane" prior to 18th May 1910 and Preston Road was renamed "Rice Lane" on 14th May 1984. Of the closed stations, the only remains are at Linacre Road where stumps of the platform supports are still visible.

Racecourse station was east of Warbreck Moor near Melling Avenue and Ford stood east of Netherton Way and south of the junction with Bridle Road. Linacre Road lay east of its namesake (north of Catherine Street) and Gladstone Dock was in an elevated position on the seaward side of the Regent Road curve approximately 200 yards from its junction with Rimrose Road. The latter station should not be confused with the Liverpool Overhead Railway "Gladstone Dock" which opened in 1930.

	Opened	Closed.
KIRKBY	20-11-1848	(still open)
FAZAKERLEY	20-11-1848	(still open)
PRESTON ROAD	20-11-1848	(still open)
RACECOURSE	c 1890	31-3-1962
FORD	1-6-1906	2-4-1951
LINACRE ROAD	1-6-1906	2-4-1951
GLADSTONE DOCK	7-9-1914	7-7-1924

Right top Kirkby looking towards Liverpool circa 1910. In the days when "best kept station" prizes were competed for it was common practice for staff to embellish an embankment or flower bed with the name of the station using white-washed bricks and stones - part of such artistry is seen here on the left. (Stations U.K.)

Right middle Fazakerley station from the west around 1910. (Stations U.K.)

Opposite bottom Preston Road (nowadays known as "Rice Lane") in Edwardian times looking towards Fazakerley. Photography in those days required large tripod cameras and relatively long exposure times. To achieve an unblurred view photographers often asked people to stand very still - it certainly appears so here but they have spoilt an otherwise excellent shot by choosing to stand to attention also! (Stations U.K.)

Top Racecourse excursion station in 1913 showing the curious "platform" arrangement with the eastbound track running through the middle of it. Its design was the solution to a number of problems that faced the company: 1. The line was on an embankment and the provision of a conventional platform would have involved expensive earthworks or supports for a station only used a couple of times a year - the returns would not have justified the cost. 2. Singling the line for a short stretch was out of the question owing to the huge volume of goods traffic throughout the year. Thus we can see why the company chose the raised and cindered trackbed arrangement - it allowed a long, wide platform for the numerous travellers, the cost of the works was minimal and the twin tracks were retained. Naturally, on race-days traffic was restricted to the westbound line for both arrivals and departures. (National Railway Museum)

Bottom left Looking east to Ford Station in 1930 showing a Liverpool Overhead Railway 3-car set on an Aintree to Dingle race-day service. (Stations U.K.)

Bottom right The single platformed Gladstone Dock station shortly after opening in 1914. It opened as a satellite of the Aintree - Marsh Lane - Liverpool Exchange service but proved unremunerative and was closed after ten years. Constructed of timber throughout and attached to a curved viaduct, its entrance was in Shore Road. (National Railway Museum)

SOUTHPORT LORD STREET - HUNTS CROSS

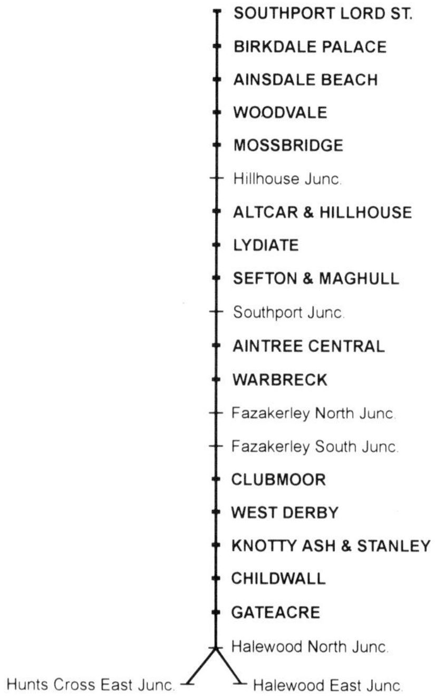

Hunts Cross East and Halewood East Junctions to Fazakerley South Junction opened in 1st December 1879 as part of the Cheshire Lines Committee Railway's North Liverpool Extension line to Walton-on-the-Hill. Fazakerley South Junction to Aintree Central first saw passengers on 13th July 1880 and the line was opened to Southport Lord Street on 1st September 1884 forming the C.L.C.'s Southport & Cheshire Lines Extension Railway.

	Opened	Closed
SOUTHPORT LORD ST.	1-9-1884	1-1-1917[1]
reopened	1-4-1919	7-1-1952
BIRKDALE PALACE	1-9-1884	1-1-1917[1]
reopened	1-4-1919	7-1-1952
AINSDALE BEACH	19-6-1901	1-1-1917[1]
reopened	1-4-1919	7-1-1952
WOODVALE	1-9-1884	1-1-1917[1]
reopened	1-4-1919	7-1-1952
MOSSBRIDGE	5-4-1886	1-1-1917
ALTCAR & HILLHOUSE	1-9-1884	1-1-1917[1]
reopened	1-4-1919	7-1-1952
LYDIATE	1-9-1884	1-1-1917[1]
reopened	1-4-1919	7-1-1952
SEFTON & MAGHULL	1-9-1884	1-1-1917[1]
reopened	1-4-1919	7-1-1952
AINTREE CENTRAL	13-7-1880	7-11-1960[2]
WARBRECK HALT [3]	1-8-1929	7-11-1960
CLUBMOOR	14-4-1927	7-11-1960
WEST DERBY	1-12-1879	7-11-1960
KNOTTY ASH & STANLEY	1-12-1879	7-11-1960
CHILDWALL	1-12-1879	1-1-1931
GATEACRE FOR WOOLTON	1-12-1879	17-4-1972

[1]Except for race-going services to Aintree on 27, 28 & 29-3-1919.

[2]Except for race-going services up to and including 3-1963.

[3]Often only used in the summer months.

Ainsdale Beach was "Seaside" prior to 1st January 1912, Woodvale "Woodville & Ainsdale" until 1st May 1898, Mossbridge "Barton & Halsall" until 1st August 1894, Sefton & Maghull "Sefton" until 1886, Knotty Ash & Stanley "Old Swan & Knotty Ash" until 1st November 1888 and Aintree Central bore the names "Aintree Racecourse" and "Aintree" prior to 1st September 1884 and 20th August 1951 respectively.

The most substantial remains are at Southport Lord Street where the frontage is still largely intact (northeast of Duke Street) and West Derby which survives as a dwelling and shop. Platform traces are still to be found at Altcar, West Derby and Knotty Ash but elsewhere there is little or no evidence of the line. Aintree Central was fairly intact until recently but a modern development now occupies the land. It is still possible to travel part of the route, albeit by car, as the trackbed from Woodvale to Birkdale Palace was utilised to support the "Coastal Road".

Birkdale Palace was west of Palace Road and sandwiched between Oxford and Weld Roads with Ainsdale Beach just north of the Shore Road / Coastal Road roundabout. Woodvale was situated at the junction of the A565 / Coastal Road and Mossbridge stood on the south side of Moss Lane by the road overbridge which lies between Haskayne and Formby. Altcar & Hillhouse was on the south side of the present Formby - Downholland road (B5195) near the sewage works and the site of Lydiate is north of Carr Lane (continuation of Station Road). Sefton & Maghull was sited south of the roadbridge on Sefton Lane and Aintree Central was south of Park Road (near Parkfield Avenue). Warbreck was south of the Walton Vale / Cedar Road junction with Clubmoor situated on the south side of Broad lane near New Hall Lane. West Derby's remains stand on Mill Lane west of the junction with Barnfield Drive and Knotty Ash was north of East Prescot Road near Chatterton Road. Childwall was on the northwest side of Well Lane and Gateacre was north of Belle Vale Road near to Belle Vue Road.

Opposite *The approaches to Southport Lord Street station in 1951 as a Class 2 4-4-0 No.40397 prepares to leave with a train for Liverpool Central. (F. Dean)*

Left top *Inside the train shed and looking towards the buffer stops at Lord Street in 1949. (Stations U.K.)*

Left bottom *Southport Lord Street from the buffers in 1949. An unusual feature of this station was the provision of a footbridge, an item not normally present or indeed necessary at a terminus. It is said by some that it was hoped that the West Lancashire Railway might junction with the Cheshire Lines Committee at Lord Street by laying a line into the latter from the north. That being so, passengers could have transferred to connecting trains via the footbridge without having to negotiate the station concourse. This might explain it to a degree but the C.L.C. would have been foolhardy to erect a large footbridge prior to the W.L.R. even seeking parliamentary approval for such a line. (Stations U.K.)*

Opposite top left Birkdale Palace from the Weld Road bridge in 1949. (Stations U.K.)

Opposite top right Ainsdale Beach station looking north in 1951. (L.G.R.P.)

Opposite middle left The southbound platform at Woodvale around the turn of the century. Note the flora throughout - this station was renowned for its manicured flowerbeds. (J. Gilmour collection)

Opposite middle right An intact but dilapidated Mossbridge as seen from the roadbridge around 1930. (J. Gilmour collection)

Opposite bottom left Looking south to Altcar & Hillhouse from Wood Lane in 1954. Although by this time closed to passengers, rail access between here and Liverpool was retained until 1960 to serve private sidings. The renowned "Altcar Bob" service from Southport (via Barton) terminated here until 1926 (see Southport Central - Hillhouse Junction chapter). (J. Thomlinson)

Opposite bottom right Lydiate from the Carr Lane level crossing in 1949. (Stations U.K.)

Above The leafy surroundings of Sefton & Maghull station in the early 1930's looking in the direction of Liverpool from the Sefton Lane bridge. (Stations U.K.)

Top left Aintree Central was equipped with one bay and four through platforms but it needed all these and more to cope with the Grand National excursion traffic. This 1930's view looking towards Southport shows the Park Road bridge in the distance. (Stations U.K.)

Top right Warbreck was the last station to be opened on the line and as will be seen in this 1930's view from the northbound platform, the usual facilities were absent. It was classed as a "halt" (an unmanned station) and was generally only used in the summer months. (Stations U.K.)

Bottom left London & North Eastern Railway class D5 No.5695 with a northbound train at Clubmoor circa 1930. "Sunday-best" seems to be the order of the day for the waiting passengers and the position and length of the shadows indicate early evening. If this is so the train can only be the ex-Gateacre 6.24 pm to Southport stopping at all stations (except Birkdale Palace) and scheduled to arrive at 7.15pm. (There were only three trains in each direction on Sundays - morning, afternoon and evening.) Third class return fares from here to Southport around that time were three shillings and nine pence. This is 18 3/4 new pence in today's currency but remember to allow for inflation - the weekly wage then was about £3. Thus, in real terms the equivalent cost today would have been approximately

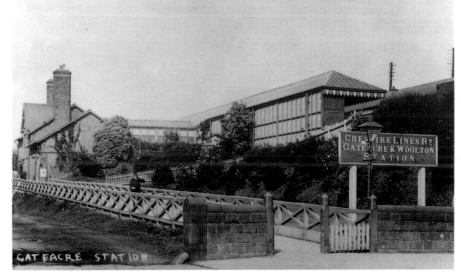

£12.50 - not as cheap as you first thought! (Stations U.K.)

Opposite bottom right Looking north to West Derby station in the late 1920's. (Stations U.K.)

Top left Knotty Ash (and Stanley) in 1954 as viewed from the north. Towards the end of the First World War the station was host to many thousands of American troops shipped through Liverpool en route for France - they were billeted at a transit camp in the adjacent Springfield Park. (H.C. Casserley)

Top right The remains of Childwall station as viewed from the north in the summer of 1949. (Stations U.K.)

Bottom left Gateacre in 1952 from the southbound platform with a train expected on the opposite line. As will be seen from the closure listing, this line died by degrees: Southport - Aintree in 1952 and Aintree - Gateacre in 1960. However, Gateacre to Hunts Cross defied the axe for another 12 years as part of the Liverpool Central - Gateacre service. (Stations U.K.)

Bottom right The exterior of Gateacre (& Woolton) in Edwardian days with its splendid nameboard facing onto Belle Vale Road. (Stations U.K.)

HUSKISSON - WALTON-ON-THE-HILL

HUSKISSON
WALTON-ON-THE-HILL
Fazakerley West Junc.
Fazakerley South Junc.
Fazakerley North Junc.

Walton-on-the-Hill to Fazakerley South Junction first saw services on 1st December 1879, Fazakerley West Junction to Fazakerley North Junction and Walton-on-the-Hill to Huskisson opened to passengers on 13th July 1880. All three were part of the Cheshire Lines Committee Railway's North Liverpool Extension line from Hunts Cross East and Halewood East Junctions. The Walton - Huskisson section differed from the rest of the North Liverpool Extension line as it lay in deep cuttings and tunnels throughout.

	Opened	Closed
HUSKISSON	13-7-1880[1]	1-5-1885
WALTON-ON-THE-HILL	1-12-1879	1-1-1918[2]

[1]For Aintree race traffic only - a regular service commenced on 2-8-1880.

[2]For regular services only - the station is known to have hosted excursion trains after this date.

The platforms of Walton-on-the-Hill and adjacent tunnel mouth were still in evidence in the early 1980's before a housing development claimed the land - the station stood northeast of the Rice Lane / Queens Drive junction. The long forgotten terminus at Huskisson was dwarfed by the surrounding massive goods depot of the same name and became part of it after passenger closure - it survived in this guise right up to complete closure of the line in 1975. The whole area has since been levelled and apart from bridge arch remains one could be forgiven for doubting that such a huge rail complex had ever existed there. The station building adjoined the north side of Boundary Street just east of Steel Street.

Above The remains of Huskisson station in 1954 by which time it had been part of the goods complex for no less than 69 years. (Stations U.K.)

Opposite Walton-on-the-Hill looking east from the top of the tunnel mouth about 1930. The engine shed of the same name is also visible at the end of the right-hand platform. (Stations U.K.)

SOUTHPORT CENTRAL - HILLHOUSE JUNCTION

SOUTHPORT CENTRAL
SOUTHPORT ASH ST.
Hawkshead St. Junc.
Meols Cop Junc.
Roe Lane Junc
MEOLS COP
BUTTS LANE HALT
Butts Lane Junc.
KEW GARDENS
HEATHEY LANE HALT
SHIRDLEY HILL
NEW CUT LANE HALT
HALSALL
PLEX MOSS LANE HALT
BARTON
Hillhouse Junc

Southport Ash Street (or Windsor Road as it was originally called) to Roe Lane Junction opened on 10th June 1878 as part of the West Lancashire Railway's line between Windsor Road and Hesketh Park - the extension to Central commenced operating on 4th September 1882. The Liverpool, Southport and Preston Junction Railway opened Roe Lane and Hawkshead Street Junctions to Hillhouse Junction on 1st November 1887 in an attempt to attract Preston to Liverpool commuters away from the Southport connection. The attempted rivalry came to nothing and both of these small companies were absorbed by the Lancashire & Yorkshire Railway in 1897, the W.L.R. on the 1st July and the L.S.& P.J.R. a fortnight later. Butts Lane Junction (to Pool Hey Junction further east) was opened on 2nd March 1911 - this section was often referred to as the Blowick Curve.

	Opened	Closed
SOUTHPORT CENTRAL	4-9-1882	1-5-1901
SOUTHPORT ASH ST.	10-6-1878	6-1902
MEOLS COP	1-11-1887	(still open)
BUTTS LANE HALT	3-1907	26-9-1938
KEW GARDENS	1-11-1887	26-9-1938
HEATHEY LANE HALT	3-1907	26-9-1938
SHIRDLEY HILL	1-11-1887	26-9-1938
NEW CUT LANE HALT	7-1906	26-9-1938
HALSALL	1-11-1887	26-9-1938
PLEX MOSS LANE HALT	7-1906	26-9-1938
BARTON	1-11-1887	26-9-1938

The line between Roe Lane Junction and site of Ash Street station became part of a new electrified service between Crossens / Southport / Liverpool on 22nd March 1904. Meols Cop to Hawkshead Street and Roe Lane Junctions was electrified on 15th February 1909 when that station was incorporated into the new service - trains calling at Meols Cop were thus required to reverse out of the station to continue the journey. This manoeuvre would have been beyond the practicality of steam engines but was easy for electric traction with motorised cars at each end.

Southport Central's services transferred to Chapel Street after closure when it became a goods depot. It stood at the junction of Derby Road and Kensington Road and survived until the 1970's when the land was redeveloped.

Southport Ash Street was originally known as "Southport Windsor Road" (being sited east of the Windsor Road footbridge) and was reduced to the rank of ticket platform with the opening of Southport Central. In 1901 the tracks were realigned to allow Preston and Barton services direct running into Chapel Street and a year later all traces of Ash Street vanished when it was superseded by St. Lukes (on the Southport - Wigan line) which was expanded to serve the Preston line also.

The Barton line (between Butts Lane Junction and Hillhouse Junction) suffered a very slow death. The section between Barton and Hillhouse Junction closed to passengers on 13th November 1926 effectively making Barton a terminus. Passenger services were withdrawn entirely on 26th September 1938 but the line lingered on for goods traffic until 21st

January 1952. This was not the complete end however, as the tracks between Shirdley Hill and Butts Lane Junction were left in for the storage of excursion rolling stock until 1964.

Butts Lane Halt was situated on the lane of the same name south of the bridge but only the tracks remain. The line survives as part of the realigned Southport - Wigan service (rerouted on 14th June 1965 between Pool Hey and St. Lukes Junctions via Meols Cop when the direct route via Blowick was closed).

Kew Gardens stood north of the A570 between Meols Cop Road and Foul Lane and was named after the nearby 12 acre park and boating lake which closed circa 1930. Heathey Lane Halt stood north of that lane (B5243) and New Cut Lane Halt

was south of the bridge where its namesake and Gregory Lane meet. Shirdley Hill was a substantive station and the only one on the branch to have a level-crossing. Its full title was "Shirdley Hill & Scarisbrick" and stood south of Renacre Lane off the A567 - the land has been redeveloped but a plaque commemorates the site. Halsall, which stood north of Carr Moss Lane survives in part as a private dwelling and the steps which led down to the halt at Plex Moss Lane (south of the bridge) were still in evidence in the late 1980's.

Barton was renamed "Downholland" on 2nd June 1924 and was situated on the south side of Station Road (off the A567 by the "Blue Bell" public house) and platform remains can still be seen. The locally-renowned "Altcar Bob" was often

photographed here and consisted of a diminutive engine and coach unit equipped with remote controls at the rear of the coach to allow reverse running - see illustration. The origin of the term "Bob" is uncertain - old railwaymen insist it was a name given to small engines generally but ex-patrons suggested it referred to the cost of a journey in early days (Bob being slang for one shilling = 5 new pence).

Opposite *The junction of Derby and Kensington Roads with a view of Southport Central exterior in 1949 after some 48 years of closure. (L.G.R.P.)*

Above *St. Lukes (Preston platforms) looking east in 1965. In 1902 this took the place of Southport Ash Street which was further west and sandwiched between Windsor and St. Lukes Roads. (Stations U.K.)*

Right top The solitary island platform at Meols Cop in 1965. The electrification, once part of the Southport - Meols Cop - Preston service, was confined to the track on the far side of the platform. (Stations U.K.)

Right bottom Kew Gardens around 1930 looking towards Southport. (J. Gilmour collection)

Opposite Shirdley Hill from the level crossing in 1949 whilst still open for goods traffic. Although freight itself had finished by 1952 tracks from Butts Lane to this point remained until 1964 for the storage of excursion stock. (Stations U.K.)

Opposite top left Halsall around 1910 looking in the direction of Barton. (J.B. Hodgson collection)

Opposite top right An extremely rare view of the "Altcar Bob" steam railmotor heading south through one of the small halts - Plex Moss Lane - about 1907. The board on the carriage roof reads "Southport, Barton, Altcar & Hillhouse". Trains did not stop at these venues unless specifically requested and the gas lamps would hopefully identify a waiting passenger to a driver after dark. There were no platforms at these tiny stopping places, just a bed of cinders and steps were lowered from the coach as required. (J. Gilmour collection)

Opposite bottom The remains of Barton station (latterly "Downholland") from the road bridge in 1949 whilst still open to occasional freight traffic - note the wagons in the distance. The line to Hillhouse Junction, disused since 1926, is seen disappearing to the right. (Stations U.K.)

Above The star of the line - the much loved "Altcar Bob" seen at Barton around 1910. Eighteen of these loco & coach units were built by the Lancashire & Yorkshire Railway (for various branches) and the one pictured here, No. 13, became L.M.S. No. 10610 after 1923. The timetable for April 1910 lists 16 trains each way on weekdays (of which 10 terminated / originated at Barton) and 9 on Sundays (8 to and from Barton). On average it took 21 & 26 minutes to cover the 6 1/2 & 9 mile journeys to Barton and Altcar respectively. This train service made such an impression on the local communities of the day that elderly residents are still writing and speaking of them - FIFTY SIX years after their passing! (G. Burgess collection)

LIVERPOOL RIVERSIDE - EDGE HILL

Edge Hill Junc

(WATERLOO GOODS)

RIVERSIDE

The line from Edge Hill to Waterloo Goods was opened for freight on 1st August 1849 and descended at a gradient of 1 in 60 for more than 2 miles. Entirely in tunnel it was worked by stationary engines until the 1890's when motive power was allowed to work through. The Mersey Docks & Harbour Board opened Riverside station on 12th June 1895 and the Waterloo line became the thoroughfare for boat trains via a dockside connection.

	Opened	Closed
LIVERPOOL RIVERSIDE	12-6-1895	25-2-1971

Sandwiched between Princes Dock and the landing stage, Riverside was demolished only recently except for a solitary wall.

Right top *A view from the buffers at Liverpool Riverside in 1950. Although not obvious from this angle, there was a track either side of the right hand platform allowing three trains at any one time. (Stations U.K.)*
Right bottom *Class 7F 0-8-0 No.49173 at Riverside in 1959 with an enthusiasts' train. (J. Hooper collection)*
Opposite *The signal box in this 1951 Edge Hill photograph is named "Waterloo Tunnel Mouth" and the opening to the right of it is where Riverside trains emerged after struggling up a 1 in 60 gradient from Waterloo Goods through more than 2 miles of tunnel. (H.C. Casserley)*

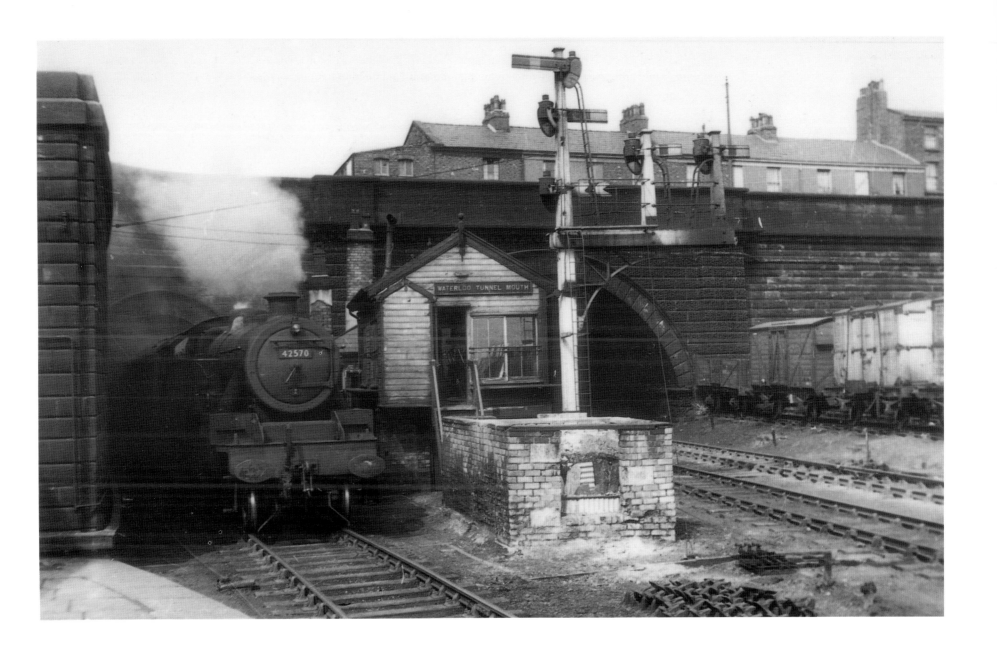

LIVERPOOL CENTRAL - BIRKENHEAD PARK & ROCK FERRY JUNCTION

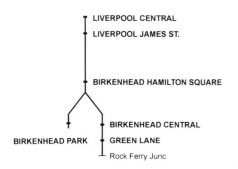

LIVERPOOL CENTRAL
LIVERPOOL JAMES ST.

BIRKENHEAD HAMILTON SQUARE

BIRKENHEAD CENTRAL

BIRKENHEAD PARK GREEN LANE

Rock Ferry Junc.

The Mersey Railway opened Liverpool James Street to Green Lane on 20th January 1886 (public services beginning on 1st February 1886) and a branch to Birkenhead Park on 2nd January 1888. This latter station was jointly owned with the Seacombe, Hoylake & Deeside (later Wirral) Railway and formed an end-on junction between the two companies. The extension to Rock Ferry first saw services on 15th June 1891 and was part owned by the Great Western and London & North Western Railways. The last section of the Mersey Railway to open was that between James Street and Liverpool Central (Low Level) on 11th January 1892. Most of the network was in tunnel, the only surface workings being the approach to Birkenhead Park, north and south of Birkenhead Central and Green Lane to Rock Ferry.

	Opened	Closed
LIVERPOOL CENTRAL	11-1-1892	28-7-1975
	reopened 9-5-1977[1]	(still open)
LIVERPOOL JAMES ST.	20-1-1886	(still open)
BIRKENHEAD HAMILTON SQ.	20-1-1886	(still open)
BIRKENHEAD CENTRAL	20-1-1886	(still open)
GREEN LANE	20-1-1886	(still open)
BIRKENHEAD PARK	2-1-1888	(still open)

[1]Reopened as part of the "Merseyrail" deep-level line which linked Central with James Street in a loop with two new stations at Moorfields (Deep-level) and Lime Street (Deep-level). The station should not be confused with the other Merseyrail station at Liverpool Central (Low-level) opened a week earlier as part of that network's Northern Line accommodating Southport - Hunts Cross and other services.

This line was the world's first under-river railway and began operations using steam locomotives fitted with condensing apparatus. They were not altogether successful and receipts were soon affected by the public's aversion to the pungent odour resulting from the action of steam on the sulphurous rock in the tunnels. Electrification came to the rescue of the company, being introduced on 3rd May 1903 and establishing another "first" - it was the country's first steam operated line to be converted to electric traction.

Apart from a long forgotten and brief period in steam days, through working between Liverpool Central - New Brighton and West Kirby was introduced on 13th March 1938 thus doing away with the need to change trains at Birkenhead Park.

The importance of the Mersey Railway cannot be overstated - it survives intact and forms the nucleus of the present Merseyrail system. Countless passengers and businesses have benefited since its excavation and without it the railway network of Merseyside would have two distinctly separate identities.

A new station at Conway Park (between Birkenhead Hamilton Square and Birkenhead Park) has been proposed but not yet acted upon.

Above The connecting staircase from Liverpool Central's concourse to its low-level Mersey Railway namesake in 1950. (Stations U.K.)

Opposite The underground station at Liverpool James Street in the 1960's - note the electric departure board with train sequence indicators top left of the picture. (Author's collection)

Right top *The exterior of Birkenhead Hamilton Square station in 1954 looking towards the river. The board above the pavement canopy reads "To Liverpool in 3 Minutes - by frequent electric trains". (H.C. Casserley)*

Right bottom *Birkenhead Central from the south in 1965 showing the additional bay platform on the right. (Stations U.K.)*

Opposite top *The dominant overhead girders cast a gloom over Green Lane in this 1965 view looking south. (Stations U.K.)*

Opposite bottom *The interchange station, Birkenhead Park, around 1930 clearly showing the two island platforms which allowed easy transfer between Mersey Railway and ex-Wirral Railway services. The latter lines (in the centre) were still steam worked at that time and terminated further on beyond Duke Street whilst the electric services were served by the platforms on the extreme left and right. Electrification was extended to West Kirby in 1938 which allowed through running as existed previously in all steam days (albeit with a change of locomotive at Birkenhead Park). (Stations U.K.)*

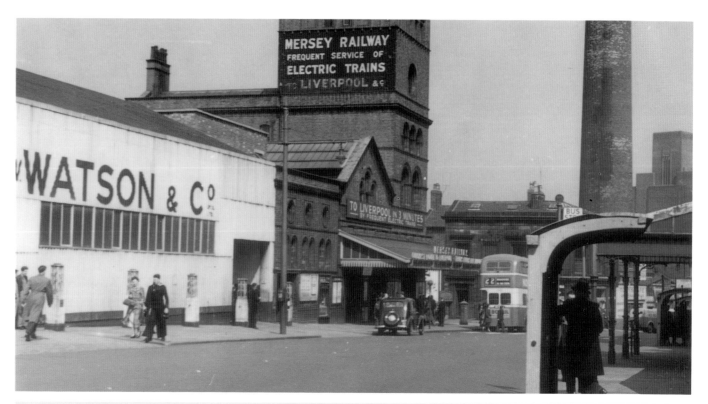

BIRKENHEAD WOODSIDE
▲ MONKS FERRY

GRANGE LANE /
BIRKENHEAD TOWN

TRANMERE
Rock Ferry Junc.
ROCK FERRY
ROCK LANE
BEBINGTON
PORT SUNLIGHT
BROMBOROUGH PORT
SPITAL
BROMBOROUGH
HOOTON
Hooton Junc.
LEDSHAM
CAPENHURST
MOLLINGTON
UPTON-BY-CHESTER
Brook Lane Junc.
Holyhead Junc.
CHESTER GENERAL

The line from Grange Lane to Chester was opened by the Chester & Birkenhead Railway on 23rd September 1840 and extended to a replacement terminus at Monks Ferry on 23rd October 1844 - the latter becoming Merseyside's first riverside station. The line was single throughout and remained so until amalgamation with the Birkenhead, Lancashire & Cheshire Junction Railway on 22nd July 1847 when provision for a second track was made. This mouthful was simplified to the Birkenhead Railway on 1st August 1859 only to be further complicated by its absorbtion into the joint Great Western and London & North Western Railways' fold on 20th November 1860. Birkenhead Woodside was opened on 31st March 1878 superseding Monks Ferry which became a coaling wharf. A further improvement was the quadrupling of the line between Birkenhead Town and Capenhurst between 1900 and 1905. The private branch to Bromborough Port was operated by the soap magnates Lever Brothers and began conveying workers on 1st May 1914.

	Opened	Closed
BIRKENHEAD		
WOODSIDE	31-3-1878	5-11-1967
MONKS FERRY	23-10-1844	31-3-1878
GRANGE LANE	23-9-1840	23-10-1844
BIRKENHEAD TOWN	23-10-1844	7- 5-1945
TRANMERE	6-1846	10-1857
ROCK FERRY	31-10-1862	(still open)
ROCK LANE	6-1846	31-10-1862
BEBINGTON	23-9-1840	(still open)
PORT SUNLIGHT	1-5-1914[1]	(still open)
BROMBOROUGH PORT	1-5-1914[2]	1929
SPITAL	c 1869	(still open)
BROMBOROUGH	c 1869	(still open)
HOOTON	23-9-1840	(still open)
LEDSHAM	23-9-1840	20-7-1959
CAPENHURST	c 1869	(still open)
MOLLINGTON	23-9-1840	7-3-1960
UPTON-BY-CHESTER	17-7-1939	9-1-1984
CHESTER GENERAL	23-9-1840	(still open)

[1]First used on 25-3-1914 for a visit by King George V. Workers' trains began 1- 5-1914. Became public station from 9-5-1927.

[2]Workers only.

Birkenhead's first station, Grange Lane, was a temporary wooden structure which stood south of its namesake (latterly Grange Street) and east of Jackson Street - it was replaced by Birkenhead Town which was built slightly east of the site and there is no evidence of either station today. The extension to the replacement terminus at Monks Ferry was in tunnel and single line throughout its existence - the station was named after the ferry which was adjacent. It stood northeast of the Church Street / Ivy Street junction but the area has been redeveloped as riverside dwellings. Birkenhead Woodside (east of the north end of Chester Street) became the eventual terminus and was built with a substantial river frontage which became something of a folly - it was originally planned that connecting ferry passengers would pass directly between the landing stage and the station. However, the ferry authorities were slow to co-operate and a "temporary" entrance was put in on the north side of the building. This became permanent by necessity when the large Woodside tram

terminus was laid north of and alongside the station in 1901 - thus, the fine buildings facing the river were never used for their intended purpose. Nothing remains of the station today, the site having become a car park.

Tranmere was originally "Lime Kiln Lane" being renamed in 1853 - the road is now named St. Pauls Road, Rock Lane (replaced by Rock Ferry further north) stood on Rock Lane West - as would be expected nothing survives of these two early closures.

Bebington was renamed "Bebington & New Ferry" on 1st May 1895 reverting to its original title on 6th May 1974. Port Sunlight opened as "Port Sunlight Halt", the suffix being dropped when it gained public status on 9th May 1927. Ledsham was known as "Sutton" prior to 1st July 1863 - it stood east of the A550 and north of the B5463 (ex-A5032) but only scant remains are visible today. The private "station" at Bromborough Port has also disappeared but there was very little to begin with - a cinder ramp near Commercial Road where employees detrained.

Mollington was situated south of the Backford - Mollington road and Upton-by-Chester lay south of Liverpool Road (A5116) a mile north of Brook Lane Junction. Nothing remains of the former station but the platforms at Upton-by-Chester are still in place.

In 1969 the quadrupled section of line between Birkenhead Town and Capenhurst was cut back to two tracks owing to a reduction in traffic.

Mersey Railway services first connected with Rock Ferry on 15th June 1891 and electrification was extended south to Hooton in 1978. The through electric service to Chester was introduced on 2nd August 1993.

New stations at Bache (south of Upton-by-Chester) and Bromborough Rake (north of Bromborough) were opened on 31st January 1984 and 30th September 1985 respectively. Another station at Eastham Rake (between Bromborough Rake and Hooton) has been proposed but not yet agreed upon at the time of writing.

Opposite An overall view of Birkenhead Woodside from the platform ends in 1960. (Stations U.K.)

Above Left Woodside from the buffer-stops in 1965 - despite the size of the station it only had five platforms as much of the lateral space was taken up by a roadway and middle tracks. (Stations U.K.)

Above Right 1947 and a rare view of the little used approach road to Birkenhead Woodside which descended from Rose Brae on the south side of the station. Virtually all patrons used the comparatively nondescript entrance on the opposite side whether on foot or connecting by car, tram or ferry. It is quite sad that such a fine Victorian awning was used for little more than harbouring mail trucks. (K.W. Green)

Opposite top left Birkenhead Town looking north in the 1930's. The site of Birkenhead's first railway station, Grange Lane, was to the left of the opposite platform beyond the canopy. (Stations U.K.)

Opposite top right Rock Ferry as viewed from the north in 1965 - lifts were housed in the three towers to assist with the transfer of mail and other goods between platforms. (Stations U.K.)

Opposite middle left An ex-Mersey Railway electric approaches Rock Ferry from the north in 1956. Passengers wishing to continue would change here for trains to Hooton and Chester. (J.A. Peden)

Opposite middle right Bebington from the south in the 1930's whilst known as "Bebington & New Ferry". (Stations U.K.)

Opposite bottom left Port Sunlight started life as a workmen's halt. This 1960 view looking north shows that it never became substantive even after gaining public status. (Stations U.K.)

Opposite bottom right A local train standing at Spital No. 1 platform in 1958. (H.B. Priestley)

Below Hooton was the major junction on the Birkenhead - Chester line being a starting point for connecting trains to West Kirby and Helsby Junction. This photograph taken from the South Signal Box shows the station in its heyday with no fewer than seven platforms. (J. Ryan collection)

Bottom left Bromborough looking towards Birkenhead around 1910. (J. Ryan collection)

Bottom right Platforms 4 and 5 at Hooton in 1956. (Stations U.K.)

Right top Ledsham station in 1960, one year after closure. (Stations U.K.)

Right bottom South of Ledsham the four tracks filtered into two as will be seen in this 1958 view of Capenhurst from the northbound platform. Class 3 2-6-2T No. 82003 working bunker first is hauling coaches ex-London Paddington on the final leg of their journey to Birkenhead Woodside. (H.B. Priestley)

Opposite top Mollington station in 1951 with a class 8F 2-8-0 about to pass through with a nouthbound goods. (Stations U.K.)

Opposite bottom Upton-By-Chester halt in 1981 looking north. (Stations U.K.)

HOOTON -
HELSBY / HELSBY & ALVANLEY

The Great Western and London & North Western Joint Railway opened a direct link between Hooton and Helsby stations on 1st July 1863 and the Cheshire Lines Committee Railway ventured north from Mouldsworth with a single line branch to Helsby & Alvanley on 1st September 1869 (Goods only). A passenger service on the latter began on 22nd June the following year and the connection to the Hooton - Helsby line was opened on 14th June 1871 to enable C.L.C. goods trains to reach Birkenhead.

	Opened	Closed
LITTLE SUTTON	1-7-1863	(still open)
ELLESMERE PORT	1-7-1863	(still open)
STANLOW &		
THORNTON	23-10-1940	(still open)
INCE & ELTON	1-7-1863	(still open)
HELSBY & ALVANLEY	22-6-1870	6-1-1964[1]

[1]Helsby & Alvanley had a curious career as a passenger station - it first closed as early as 1-5-1875 and was not reopened until October 1936 when it was used occasionally. It closed again on 22-5-1944 but was reinstated on 9-9-1963 to commence its last and shortest period of public service - less than 4 months!

Little Sutton first opened as "Sutton" being renamed on 19th October 1886, Ellesmere Port was known as "Whitby Locks" prior to 1st September 1870 and Ince & Elton was simply "Ince" before 17th April 1884. Stanlow & Thornton began life as a private halt for workers at the Shell oil refinery which surrounds the site - it gained public status on 24th February 1941.

The Helsby & Alvanley line was taken out of use entirely on 14th September 1991 but much of the ex-C.L.C. station remains - situated east of the A56 road overbridge, the platform is intact and the building serves as a private dwelling.

A new station, Overpool, situated between Little Sutton and Ellesmere Port was opened on 15th August 1988.

Opposite top Little Sutton from the east in 1960 - note the tiny signal box on the left. (H.C. Casserley)

Opposite middle Ellesmere Port station looking towards the level crossing in the 1930's. (Stations U.K.)

Opposite bottom Looking east from the footbridge at Stanlow & Thornton in 1971 amidst the massive oil refinery. (Stations U.K.)

Left top Ince & Elton from the roadbridge in 1971 with the Ince electric generating station visible beyond the station buildings. (Stations U.K.)

Left bottom The C.L.C. single platformed station at Helsby & Alvanley as viewed from the A56 roadbridge in 1949. This station had a very chequered career - in the 94 years between opening and final closure it only served the public for 13 of them! (Stations U.K.)

HOOTON - WEST KIRBY

West Kirby Junc.
WEST KIRBY (B.J.R.)
KIRBY PARK
CALDY
THURSTASTON
HESWALL
PARKGATE
NESTON
HADLOW ROAD
Hooton Junc.

The Great Western and London & North Western Joint Railways continued their exploration of the Wirral with another branch line from Hooton, this time to Parkgate. Single line throughout (with passing loops at some stations), it opened on 1st October 1866 and was extended to West Kirby on 19th April 1886.

	Opened	Closed
HADLOW ROAD	1-10-1866	17-9-1956
NESTON	1-10-1866	17-9-1956
PARKGATE (1st Station)	1-10-1866	19-4-1886
PARKGATE (2nd Station)	19-4-1886	17-9-1956
HESWALL	19-4-1886	17-9-1956
THURSTASTON	19-4-1886	1-2-1954
CALDY	5-1909	1-2-1954
KIRBY PARK	10-1894	5-7-1954
WEST KIRBY	19-4-1886	17-9-1956[1]

[1]To public services only, personnel from a nearby Air Force base continued to use the station after this date. The line continued with Goods services until complete closure on 7th May 1962.

Neston was renamed "Neston South" on 15th September 1952. Parkgate's first station, a single track terminus, became a goods depot when the second and larger station (with passing loop) was built further north upon extending the line to West Kirby. Passing loops with two platforms were also a feature of Hadlow Road, Heswall and Thurstaston stations.

Most of Hadlow Road station has been preserved and is worth a visit. Situated at Hadlow Road, Willaston, it is a good starting point for those wishing to explore the "Wirral Way" - the trackbed of the entire line, once overgrown but now made passable for hikers and cyclists (bar a few gaps caused by redevelopment and bridge removals).

Elsewhere, remains are far less evident. Neston stood west of Mellock Lane and south of Station Road but houses now occupy the site. Parkgate lay to the north of Station Road and east of Ropewalk but all that exists are traces of the subway and sloping footpath. Heswall stood south of Station Road but although the area has seen redevelopment one of the buildings survives as a private dwelling. Thurstaston was situated south of yet another Station Road and platform supports are still in existence. Caldy was north of Croft Drive and inland of the line but nothing has survived. Kirby Park stood north of Sandy Lane and west of Ludlow Drive - the only clue that remains is a notice board by the bridge. The joint line station at West Kirby was another redevelopment casualty. It lay north of Grange Road and east of the present (ex-Wirral Railway) terminus - an access road was opposite Westbourne Road.

Opposite top Hadlow Road from the level crossing about 1950. (Stations U.K.)

Opposite middle Looking west to Neston, about 1939 as a Hooton bound train draws to a halt. (Stations U.K.)

Opposite bottom Parkgate (2nd station) viewed from the south in 1960. The passing loop here necessitated two platforms and access between them was via a subway, the arched roof of which can just be seen between the rails further on. (Stations U.K.)

Left top Heswall 4 years after passenger closure looking towards Station Road. (Stations U.K.)

Left bottom Thurstaston in 1946 looking south from the roadbridge. As with Parkgate and Heswall, two platforms were provided to accommodate the loop line. Originally, Thurstaston had a solitary platform - the one on the right of this picture (together with loop) was added later. Note that this and the two stations further north closed to passengers before the others - see dates. (Stations U.K.)

Above *Pure nostalgia - Class 51XX 2-6-2T No. 5186 pulls into Caldy station with a northbound train in 1953. (Stations U.K.)*

Opposite top *Kirby Park station looking north from Sandy Lane bridge in 1953. (Stations U.K.)*

Opposite bottom left *West Kirby Joint line station from a southern viewpoint in the late 1920's. It was known as "the joint" locally to distinguish it from the ex-Wirral Railway terminus of the same name situated nearby. A study of this view is a lesson in what rail travel was like in its heyday, even on such a minor line - the stationmaster in his frock-coat keeping a watchful eye; the guard with his handlamp and other trappings of office; reflections from gleaming coaches; wrought iron benches complete with station name; a mailcart ready to assist with the transport of any trunks; last "good-byes" through those leather belted carriage windows; a gentleman in jodhpurs and his young charge wait for the engine to be attached - alas, those days are gone forever. (Stations U.K.)*

Opposite bottom right *Looking south from West Kirby in 1954 as class 14XX 0-4-2T No.1457 replenishes its tanks at the water tower. (R.M. Casserley)*

The Hoylake Railway (known as the Hoylake and Birkenhead Rail & Tramway Company from 18th July 1872, the Seacombe, Hoylake & Deeside Railway from 18th July 1881 and latterly the Wirral Railway from 1st July 1891) opened Birkenhead Docks to Hoylake on 2nd July 1866 with extensions to West Kirby and Birkenhead North on 1st April 1878. The same company continued the line to an end on junction with the Mersey Railway at Birkenhead Park on 2nd January 1888. It was a single line with passing loops at Moreton and Hoylake until Birkenhead Park to Hoylake was doubled in 1895 continuing to West Kirby in 1896. Third-rail electrification and through running to Liverpool Central Low Level was introduced on 14th March 1938.

	Opened	Closed
BIRKENHEAD NORTH	1-4-1878	(still open)
BIRKENHEAD DOCKS	2-7-1866	1-1-1870[1]
	reopened 1-8-1872[3]	1-4-1878
BIDSTON	2-7-1866	1-1-1870[1]
	reopened 1-8-1872[3]	6-1890
	5-1896	(still open)
LEASOWE	1-1-1870[2]	1-8-1872[3]
	5-5-1894[4]	(still open)
MORETON	2-7-1866	(still open)
MEOLS	2-7-1866	(still open)
MANOR ROAD	14-3-1938	(still open)
HOYLAKE	2-7-1866	(still open)
WEST KIRBY (1st Station)	1-4-1878	1896
WEST KIRBY (2nd Station)	1896[5]	(still open)

[1]Caused by bankruptcy of the line and subsequent seizure of the portion between Leasowe and Birkenhead Docks.

[2]Became a temporary terminus (without buildings) at a level crossing owing to above seizure.

[3]When normal services resumed.

[4]As a purpose-built station.

[5]Replaced the 1st station upon doubling of the line.

Birkenhead North was originally named "Birkenhead Docks" taking the name from the 1866 station further north which it replaced. The original Birkenhead Docks station was opened as "Docks" but it was also known as Wallasey Bridge Road on occasions - it officially became Birkenhead Docks on 1st August 1872. Leasowe was known as "Leasowe Crossing" up to 1st August 1872.

The 1938 electrification resulted in a new station at Manor Road and the rebuilding of Bidston, Leasowe, Moreton, Meols, Hoylake and West Kirby (2nd).

Birkenhead Docks (1866 station) was approximately 11 chains northwest of Birkenhead North and nothing remains. Upon closure the original station at West Kirby became a joint goods shed with the G.W.R./L.N.W.R. line nearby but closed completely on 30th October 1965 - the site, which stood east of the 2nd station, has since been reclaimed.

Opposite *Birkenhead North around 1939 shortly after electrification. (Stations U.K.)*
Above *Lines from Bidston led to the four points of the compass, north to New Brighton, south to Hawarden, east to Birkenhead and west to West Kirby. This photograph taken circa 1939 looks west and shows the junction of the ex-G.C.R. and ex-Wirral lines beyond the station. (Stations U.K.)*
Left *Leasowe station in the Edwardian era. (J. Ryan collection)*

Right Moreton looking east from the Birkenhead platform about 1905. Note the economic facilities - these were a legacy of the line's early financial troubles. (J. Ryan collection)

Below Meols shortly after electrification and rebuilding. (Stations U.K.)

Opposite top left Manor Road looking towards Birkenhead in 1960. This station was added in 1938 as part of the electrification programme. (Stations U.K.)

Opposite top right An elevated view of the original station at Hoylake taken from the gasworks around 1905. The inordinate number of advertising signs and different styles of building gave it a somewhat ramshackle appearance. (J. Ryan collection)

Opposite bottom Hoylake circa 1939 after rebuilding. (Stations U.K.)

THE STATION FROM THE BRIDGE · WEST KIRBY

The approaches to West Kirby (2nd Station - Wirral Rly.) as seen from Bridge Road about 1905. The lines curving left in the foreground connected with the joint G.W.R./L.N.W.R. station of the same name which was situated nearby. (Stations U.K.)

West Kirby (2nd Station - ex-Wirral Rly) as rebuilt and looking towards the buffers circa 1939. (Stations U.K.)

BIDSTON -
NEW BRIGHTON / SEACOMBE

Bidston Junctions to Wallasey Grove Road was opened by the Seacombe, Hoylake & Deeside Railway (known as the Wirral Railway after 1st July 1891) on 2nd January 1888 to be quickly followed by the extension to New Brighton on 30th March the same year. The same company opened the secondary branch to Seacombe on 1st June 1895. Bidston to New Brighton received third-rail electrification on 14th March 1938.

	Opened	Closed
WALLASEY VILLAGE	1907	(still open)
WALLASEY GROVE ROAD	2-1-1888	(still open)
WARREN	30-3-1888	1-10-1916
NEW BRIGHTON	30-3-1888	(still open)
LISCARD & POULTON	1-6-1895	4-1-1960
SEACOMBE	1-6-1895	4-1-1960

Wallasey Village opened as "Leasowe Road" but had been renamed by 1909 and Wallasey Grove Road was originally "Wallasey" prior to 31st May 1948. Warren began life as "Warren Park" but lost the suffix by 1891 and Seacombe was renamed "Seacombe & Egremont" on 1st July 1901 only to revert back on 5th January 1953.

Wallasey Village and New Brighton were rebuilt in 1938 as part of the electrification scheme.

Warren was an early closure as there were few patrons other than golfers - it was situated just east of Sea Road and there are no traces remaining today.

Passenger receipts from the Seacombe branch were never good and its demise was hinted at when excluded from the electrification programme. Mostly cut from rock, the line would have been a costly addition to the company's route miles had the goods traffic not proved so good. However, the final nail in the coffin was driven home on 17th June 1963 when the branch closed completely. Liscard station was situated in a cutting west of Mill Lane but all traces disappeared during construction of the Kingsway Mersey Tunnel / M53 approach road which took advantage of the ready made excavation, followed much of its course and widened it further. The site of Seacombe has also succumbed to redevelopment in the form of flats situated northwest of the junction between Church and Borough Roads.

and this is no exception - note that there are no less than three gentlemen wearing top hats. A horse drawn coach waiting to convey its well-to-do owner completes this period scene. (Stations U.K.)

Top right Looking towards the buffers at New Brighton in 1950 with an ex-L.M.S. electric waiting to depart - the platform shelters were added during the modernisation programme. Not many realise that between 1923 & 1939 it was possible to travel between here and London Euston without changing trains. Connecting coaches operated via Bidston, West Kirby (Joint Stn.), Hooton and Crewe with slight delays at the last two venues whilst they were attached to other trains. (Stations U.K.)

Left Another early view of New Brighton, this time from the buffers and shortly after the arrival of an eight coach train. The locomotive has stopped short of the crossover so it can uncouple and run round the carriages. (J. Ryan collection)

Opposite top Wallasey Village station in 1950 looking towards Bidston. Rebuilt in 1938 as part of the ex-Wirral Railway electrification and modernisation programme, note that the style was identical with those upgraded elsewhere (compare with Meols & Hoylake on the West Kirby branch). (Stations U.K.)

Opposite middle A track level view of Wallasey Grove Road in 1950. (Stations U.K.)

Opposite bottom Warren, so named after the nearby golf course, taken after closure from Sea Road bridge. (L.G.R.P.)

Top left The frontage that once graced New Brighton with a sign that left strangers under no illusion as to the purpose of the building. The presence of a photographer in Edwardian times usually led to an impromptu gathering

Right top *Liscard & Poulton station looking east to the Mill Road bridge about 1930. Although not quite apparent from this angle, the platform was of the island type with a track on the far side also. As reported in the main text, this site is now occupied by the Kingsway Mersey Tunnel / M53 road connection. (Stations U.K.)*

Right bottom *Seacombe (& Egremont) on a sunny Edwardian morning with a throng of day-trippers heading towards the exit. This station was equipped with three platforms to cope with the extra traffic that the nearby ferry connection generated. (Stations U.K.)*

Opposite top *The distant Liver Building is just visible in this 1920's view of Seacombe as workmen toil with repairs to the crude wooden platform. (Stations U.K.)*

Opposite bottom *Looking west to a ghost-like Seacombe a few months after passenger closure in 1960. Compare this photograph with the bustling Edwardian scene - gone forever are the hurrying commuters and excited trippers. (Stations U.K.)*

BIDSTON - CHESTER LIVERPOOL ROAD

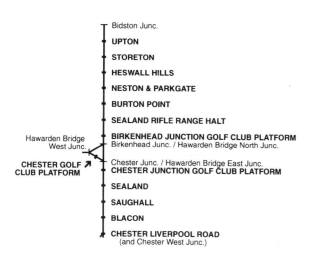

Bidston Junc.
UPTON
STORETON
HESWALL HILLS
NESTON & PARKGATE
BURTON POINT
SEALAND RIFLE RANGE HALT
BIRKENHEAD JUNCTION GOLF CLUB PLATFORM
Birkenhead Junc. / Hawarden Bridge North Junc.

Hawarden Bridge West Junc.

CHESTER GOLF ↗ CLUB PLATFORM
Chester Junc. / Hawarden Bridge East Junc.
CHESTER JUNCTION GOLF CLUB PLATFORM
SEALAND
SAUGHALL
BLACON
CHESTER LIVERPOOL ROAD
(and Chester West Junc.)

Below *Upton from the south in 1960. Although open today and still double line the original buildings have gone in favour of the all too common "bus-stop" appearance. (Stations U.K.)*

Opposite *A postcard view of the northbound platform at Upton in August 1914 showing a cheerful group of soldiers posing for the camera. One can't help wondering how many of these brave young lions perished in the terrible conflict that lay ahead. (J. Ryan collection)*

Chester Junctions to Hawarden Bridge West Junction was opened on 31st March 1890 by the Manchester, Sheffield & Lincolnshire Railway (known as the Great Central Railway from 1st August 1897). Bidston Junction to Hawarden Bridge Junctions first opened to goods traffic on 16th March 1896 with passenger services commencing on 18th May the same year - it was the joint concern of the Manchester, Sheffield & Lincolnshire and Wrexham, Mold & Connah's Quay Railways (this undertaking was otherwise known as the Dee & Birkenhead Committee becoming the North Wales & Liverpool Railway Committee from 7th August 1896 - it was eventually absorbed by the Great Central Railway on 1st January 1905).

	Opened	Closed
UPTON	18-5-1896	(still open)
STORETON		
(for BARNSTON)	18-5-1896	3-12-1951
HESWALL HILLS	1-5-1898	(still open)
NESTON & PARKGATE	18-5-1896	(still open)
BURTON POINT	1-8-1899	5-12-1955
SEALAND		
RIFLE RANGE HALT	pre 6-1923	14-6-1954
BIRKENHEAD JUNC.		
GOLF CLUB PLATFORM	5-1896	post 1923
CHESTER GOLF		
CLUB PLATFORM	1891	1895[1]
CHESTER JUNC.		
GOLF CLUB PLATFORM	1895[2]	pre 7-1923
SEALAND	post 1915[3]	9-9-1968
SAUGHALL	31-3-1890	1-2-1954
BLACON	31-3-1890	9-9-1968
CHESTER		
LIVERPOOL ROAD	31-3-1890	3-12-1951

[1]The building of the Hawarden Junctions triangle necessitated closure. It was replaced by Chester Junction Golf Club Platform further east.

[2]Replaced Chester Golf Club Platform (see [1] also).

[3]For the use of military personnel - it gained public status c 1919.

Storeton was known as "Barnston" prior to 1st November 1897 becoming "Storeton for Barnston" later and Heswall Hills was renamed "Heswall" on 7th May 1973.

Neston & Parkgate underwent two name changes, to "Neston North" on 15th September 1952 and "Neston" on 6th May 1968. Sealand's original title was "Welsh Road Halt" being renamed on 14th September 1931.

Storeton was situated north of Station Road but there are no traces remaining today. Burton Point is virtually intact north of Station Road, Burton, except for slight dilapidation and the removal of the footbridge and platform edging. Sealand Rifle Range has disappeared completely, it stood approximately 1 mile 25 chains south of Burton Point. Nothing remains of the three golf club halts that once existed by the Hawarden Junctions triangle; Birkenhead Junction Golf Club platform was situated 2 chains north of its namesake; Chester Golf Club Platform was a few chains east of Hawarden Bridge West Junction (on the Chester line) and its successor, Chester Junction Golf Club Platform was east of its namesake by a similar margin. An industrial estate has swallowed up the site of Sealand station which stood at map reference SJ 331701. Saughall was east of Seahill Road as was Blacon on Saughall Road - platforms can still be seen at both locations. All traces of Chester Liverpool Road have gone, it was situated west of Liverpool Road at its junction with Brook Lane.

Bidston to Hawarden Bridge West Junction is still open to passenger traffic with three of the stations having survived as will be seen from the accompanying table. Chester East and South Junctions to Hawarden Bridge West and North Junctions closed to passengers on 9th September 1968 and goods on 20th April 1984 but reopened as a single line for goods from Dee Marsh Junction (previously known as Hawarden Bridge North Junction) to Mickle Trafford on 31st August 1986. It has since lost any regular traffic but the line remains in situ for emergency use.

"Upton Station" August 1914

C.R.J. Wirral Series.
Greasby, Ches.

11

Opposite top left *Looking north to Storeton (for Barnston) from the road bridge in 1946. (Stations U.K.)*

Opposite top right *Class 2 2-6-2T No.41237 calls at Heswall Hills in 1957 with a Seacombe to Wrexham train. (H.B. Priestley)*

Opposite middle left *Neston & Parkgate from the south in 1960 during its "Neston North" period. (Stations U.K.)*

Opposite middle right *Burton Point from the Station Road overbridge in 1953 - as with Storeton, its inconvenient position led to early closure. (Stations U.K.)*

Opposite bottom left *Sealand looking west in 1951. (Stations U.K.)*

Opposite bottom right *Class C13 4-4-2T No.67433 eases a Chester-bound train into Saughall in 1951. (Stations U.K.)*

Left top *The method of white-washing platform ends is shown in this 1951 view of Blacon. A long handled brush was used with a plank to provide a straight edge. (Stations U.K.)*

Left bottom *Chester Liverpool Road from the bridge of the same name around 1930. The station was situated in the fork of Chester West Junction which is visible in the distance. The platforms nearest the camera are for Chester Northgate services whilst those beyond accommodated any trains avoiding the city. (Stations U.K.)*

CHESTER GENERAL - HELSBY

```
┴  HELSBY and Helsby Junc.
┼  DUNHAM HILL
┼  MICKLE TRAFFORD (B.J.R.)
   Mickle Trafford Junc.
┼  Manchester Junc. / Chester No.1 Junc.
┴  (CHESTER GENERAL)
```

Chester General to Manchester Junction was opened on 1st October 1840 as part of the Grand Junction Railway's line between Chester and Crewe - this company was one of the three which became the London & North Western Railway on 16th July 1846. Manchester Junction to Helsby first saw services on 18th December 1850 as part of a line built by the Birkenhead, Lancashire and Cheshire Junction Railway between Chester and Warrington - this company became known as the Birkenhead Railway from 1st August 1859 and was absorbed by the Great Western and London & North Western joint Railways on 20th November 1860.

	Opened	Closed
MICKLE TRAFFORD (B.J.R.)	12-1889	2-4-1951
DUNHAM HILL	18-12-1850	7-4-1952
HELSBY	1852	(still open)

Dunham Hill was originally known as "Dunham" being renamed in April 1861. Mickle Trafford stood south of the lane which connects the village of the same name with Guilden Sutton - there are no traces today although the line is open for through services. The same is true for Dunham Hill which was situated south of the Thornton-le-Moors to Dunham on the Hill road. The junctions at Helsby and Mickle Trafford were opened on 1st July 1863 and 4th October 1942 respectively.

Opposite top *The Birkenhead Joint Railway station at Mickle Trafford from the Warrington platform in 1949. The rails on the extreme left were a 1942 war-time connection with the nearby C.L.C. line - note the ballast has not yet discoloured. Its provision necessitated rebuilding the Chester platform further south - compare the platform surfaces, the northbound is of original timber construction whilst the opposite is cinders with concrete edging. The closure of Chester Northgate in 1969 saw this junction reversed so that ex-C.L.C. services could use Chester General. Later, a scissor crossing was put it in which allowed connections either way. (Stations U.K.)*

Opposite bottom *Dunham Hill from the roadbridge in 1949. (Stations U.K.)*

Left top *Looking northeast along the Chester - Warrington platforms (nos. 1 & 2) at Helsby Junction about 1930. The nameboard of the left advises "change for Ince & Elton, Ellesmere Port and Little Sutton". (Stations U.K.)*

Left bottom *An overall view of Helsby Junction in 1971 showing the Hooton lines branching to the right through platforms 3 & 4. Note that the footbridge had lost its roof by this year. (Stations U.K.)*

CHESTER NORTHGATE - BARROW FOR TARVIN

Chester Northgate to Barrow for Tarvin opened on 2nd November 1874 (goods only) as part of the Cheshire Lines Committees course between Chester and Mouldsworth - passenger services did not commence until 1st May 1875.

	Opened	Closed
CHESTER NORTHGATE	1-5-1875	6-10-1969
MICKLE TRAFFORD		
(C.L.C.)	1-5-1875	12-2-1951
BARROW FOR TARVIN	1-5-1875	1-6-1953

Mickle Trafford was renamed "Mickle Trafford East" on 5th June 1950 and Barrow for Tarvin was known as "Tarvin & Barrow" prior to November 1883.

Chester Northgate disappeared completely when the site was redeveloped for the Northgate Arena complex. Any evidence of Mickle Trafford has also been erased but the station building at Barrow for Tarvin has survived as a private dwelling. Mickle Trafford was sited north of the lane which connects that village with Guilden Sutton whilst Barrow lay west of the B5132 near Little Barrow.

Through passenger services still operate but the closure of Chester Northgate necessitated their diversion to Chester General via Mickle Trafford Junction. The section from Mickle Trafford to Chester Liverpool Road (and through to Hawarden) was singled and retained for goods but this traffic has since been lost - however, the line is still in situ for emergency purposes.